DETAILS
AT 10

DETAILS
AT 10

BEHIND THE HEADLINES OF
TEXAS TELEVISION HISTORY

BERT N. SHIPP

Charleston THE London
History
PRESS

Published by The History Press
Charleston, SC 29403
www.historypress.net

Copyright © 2011 by Bert Shipp
All rights reserved

First published 2011

Manufactured in the United States

ISBN 978.1.60949.415.5

Shipp, Bert.
Details at ten : behind the headlines of Texas television history / Bert Shipp.
p. cm.
ISBN 978-1-60949-415-5
1. Shipp, Bert. 2. Television journalists--Texas--Biography. 3. Television broadcasting of
news--Texas--History--20th century. I. Title.
PN4874.S4765A3 2011
070.4'3--dc23
2011032148

Contents

CONTENTS

Acknowledgements

I have debts I can never pay to the departed television news pioneers James Byron, Doyle Vinson, Tom McDonald, Jim Murray, Dan Owens, Jim Kerr and Mike Shapiro.

My best to Russ Thornton, Bob Welch and Jimmy Darnell, colleagues who shared many exciting years.

Volumes of thanks to Janie Bryan Loveless, who edited and revised all the various drafts of this book.

Thanks, too, to Liz Oliphant, without whose counsel and dedication to the product this book would not have been possible.

Bless you Ann Trees, Murphy Martin and Brett Shipp for reviewing a world of words and offering wise advice to make the stories better.

And, finally, all my love to Shan, who says, "What book?"

Introduction

M ost books need a little explaining—an introduction, if you will. The author can forestall such questions as, "What is this book about?" and, "Why did you write it?" Fair questions, both. So in this introduction, I can tell how I got to my exalted television news position, showing how my progress up the television ladder parallels the growth of the industry itself. My book can become a history of sorts, with a personal flavor.

This book is not about the slick, technologically sophisticated, computer-driven operation that the television news industry has become. Instead, I've chronicled true stories about the birth and early childhood, if you will, of one of the most pervasive electronic forces in our lives and of the news people who created it. These are stories of the development of television news in the '50s and '60s. Newspapers were still king, but the new kid on the block was gradually being recognized.

In Dallas/Fort Worth, local television news was born in the '50s. Actually, like the number of channels, the hours of broadcasting were fairly limited. The programming and staging of news, dramatic presentations and even product advertising were mostly literal and straightforward. The fact that anything at all showed up on the screen was probably a cause for wonder and entertainment to the viewer.

The Federal Communications Commission (FCC), the government's watchdog on every aspect of the communications industry, mandated that a station had to provide some programming in the public interest to keep its license. TV station managers discovered that news was a public service. And, happy day, it was a tax write-off.

But in an industry rich in writing talent and investigative reporting know-how, who knew how to "do" television news? Who knew how to present what was essentially a picture story in an interesting way for the audience while still preserving the integrity of the story? What, if any, was the difference between print and electronic journalism?

Back then, journalism classes paid little attention to television and radio news. Southern Methodist University's journalism professors, such as the inimitable Tom Simmons, the astute E.L. Callihan and stalwart Martin Sylvester Reese, concluded their twelve-week classes on producing a newspaper with the airy opinion from the journalism textbook, noting how "much of the contents of this book can be applied to the field of radio and television." That was it.

Newspapers and radio reporters really had it easy. Newspaper reporters interviewed the people involved in their stories, and their photographers shot the pictures, usually after the fact.

Radio newsmen used words to "picture the news." They just had to be on the scene sometime before the principals left. They'd shove a mike in someone's face and roll the audio tape. If the subject's quotes didn't say what the reporter needed for the story, the reporter would simply roll the tape until somebody said something memorable. And audio tape was so quick and easy to edit.

Television was different. In these stories of the '50s, my colleagues and I had to be where the news was happening. We needed the action live, and live action, like life itself, stops for no one. Burdened with heavy equipment and the ubiquitous notebook, we raced to the scene of a story, mentally composing pictures and words in our heads. And it was so in real life.

News soldiers of the '50s, like Ken Martin, Jim Murray, Wayne Brown, Dan Owens, Jimmy Kerr, Joe Dave Scott, George Sanderson, Forrest Moore and Wes Wise, attacked their subjects armed with the venerable 16mm Bell & Howell and the ever-forgiving Cinevoice sound camera. Some lens hawks used and maintained a stylistic camera known as a Bolex. They figured out the difference between print and electronic journalism in telling the story. They knew how to make that story come alive with real-life pictures, the sound of real-life voices and the incredible vibrancy of witnessing something happening right now. If they "staged" a picture occasionally or made a small fire look like a conflagration, they didn't alter the reality—they only provided what their audience demanded: the immediacy of the action.

You can't discuss the early days of television news in the Dallas–Fort Worth market without hearing the names of WBAP-TV Channel 5's master splicers on the editing bench, as well as experts in the art of the rewrite—Doyle Vinson, Tom McDonald, Russ Thornton, Charles Murphy and Clint Bourland. They were giants, the best in the business. They knew what they were doing because they had figured out what the new medium demanded. They made a lot of news guys look good as they cleaned up material tossed in from the field.

The godfather was James E. Byron, a veteran of the *Fort Worth Star Telegram* newsroom. He was news director of WBAP and manager of *The Texas News*, acknowledged in the industry as the best news operation anywhere. When books and articles chronicle the advancements made in the field of television journalism, Byron's name is always there. He brought the canons of journalism to television news that still form the bedrock of the industry.

I had the privilege of working with Mr. Byron for two years. I was almost ashamed and disheartened to approach him with the news that I would be leaving the treasured *Texas News* operation. I loved the work and the people, but most of all, I was proud to be associated with the number one news producer in the Southwest. The worst part of telling him was my embarrassment in admitting that I was leaving for a higher position and, of all things, *more money*! Oh, the shame of it all! Such an attitude seems very quaint and naïve now, but Byron certainly was worth working for to more newsmen than me. A measure of the man lies in his reaction to my news. He simply set me at ease, telling me that he figured I'd be leaving before long. "Because," he said, "you learned too fast and too well. Your strength is in your desire to do your best." What a send-off!

James Byron defined and guided the TV news industry from its first stumbling steps. For years, in the pressure cooker of a chaotic news day, when I would be tempted to cut corners or stretch the truth, I could hear a caution from "Lord" Byron. Every time we went on assignment, we were writing or rewriting the book on television news. When we made mistakes, we tried to learn from them.

I am glad that I lasted long enough to see television journalism grow up. In many ways, it has overtaken its big brother, the newspaper. Today's universities have a variety of offerings to attract young people to what are now called media courses. Television news now draws more people than periodicals or newspapers. And the pay is very good and only getting better.

But this was the way it was in the television news industry of the '50s and '60s. The stories are all true, and the characters are real. It was a wonderful time to be young and working in such an exciting field. I hope this book helps all of us remember when television news was new and still a work in progress.

To write "-30-" to this memoir, I'll quote my favorite newscaster, Murphy Martin, who always closed his evening report with, "That's my time, thank you for yours."

The Toad-Tough Lady

The fire was starting to white out. Only a minute ago it was a hostile black finger of smoke picking at a scab of midmorning smog that crusted the air over the cheap streets of Northwest Dallas.

The disappearing flames were also vaporizing any thoughts I had that a good fire story might get me an early entry on the WBAP-TV Channel 5 daily news assignment board. A reporter had to make his mark quickly on the board or he'd end up at a boring city council meeting, or worse. (Worse was the county commissioners' doubly-dull semicircle of seated dry rot). Or he could be dispatched to the bottoms along the Trinity River, where there's not a breeze to be bought and chiggers are as thick as the layer of stench oozing from the decomposed carcass of a wino who had missed roll call at the Buckhorn bar for a week or two.

As a WBAP Bureau news chaser, I was excited to watch the towering flames propel plumes of heavy smoke skyward. This roaring house fire had all the get-up-and-go it takes to hoist an average news story up to maybe even lead a newscast. Brilliant flames and a squad of hustling firemen were just what it took to satisfy the demands of a picky editor.

"Ya gotta hook 'em early," the pit bosses counseled. "If a viewer's interest isn't snared in the first ten seconds of a news story, you can kiss 'em goodbye. Those fickle fans are off to the pot or the pad." That was according to the small print in the ratings logs.

I had only been in the television business about a year, but with five years as a Dallas newspaper reporter, I was no neophyte when it came to fires or violence. But here, with the flames growing weak, it didn't take an experienced newsman to figure that water had met wood and water had won.

"Crap!" I muttered under my breath. But at least my New Year's resolution to stop using foul language kept a stronger expletive muffled and this utterance short but decent.

A few minutes earlier, up around Joe Field Circle, known as the most dangerous traffic spot in Dallas, I had a close call. I came within a horn honk of getting clobbered by a careless motorist. If that had happened seven months ago, I would have cursed the driver to the limit as a "low-life, liver-lipped, no-good, extra rotten somma' bitch." But today I was still trying to keep at least this New Year's resolution to "quit my rude, crude cussin." I figured that if I was going to try to keep just one vow, a no-swearing oath ought to be a doable endeavor. So the "low-life, liver-lipped, no-good, extra-rotten somma' bitch" came out a more respectable, "You low-grade, careless driver!"

What really irked me, though, was that my brand-spankin'-new orange Opel wagon of German ancestry got its first ding. Not a real dent, but the front license plate now had its first traffic scar. My insides still churned, but not entirely from the frightening encounter.

Actually, I hated to admit it, even to myself, but some of that queasy feeling could be attributed to a bit of misbehavior the night before. I had overserved myself (another New Year's resolution shot to hell) at the grand opening of a new tire shop down on Industrial Boulevard. Unfortunately, I had a thing for tire shops and had developed a deep devotion to those that opened for business with a tub of very cold beer and a wide variety of cold cuts.

The best I could remember, I had spent much of the evening offering toasts to all the brands of tires I could think of. I even hoisted a brew in honor of one or two brands long since discontinued. Wonder what ever happened to old favorites such as Fisk and Sieberling?

Alas, today I fought off the fear of being the last newsman to the fast-cooling fire, while I wondered how long it would be before I quit regretting last evening's antics. In my pre–New Year's resolution days, I was no stranger to the "hall of hangovers." Right now, I longed for a bicarbonate of soda. It would not only improve the system, it would also level the disposition.

Looking at the gray smoke spiraling skyward from the fire call over on Sylvester Street, I realized that my opportunity to film flames had been snuffed out. No flames meant a weaker story. Losing time at the traffic circle was a real setback. I fervently wished someone would invent Alka-Seltzer in a tablet like Tums. The fizz would set a fella free.

While I was preoccupied with the uncertain state of my health, I had been ignoring the real object of my midmorning consternation, right in the seat beside me. The occupant was a first-day newcomer to the TV news operation. His name was Bob Crowe, and he was just a door-slam out of North Texas State University's "J" school. He smelled as though he had bathed in something you could get at Ward's drugstore on sale, called Brut. It was brutal all right.

The bureau chief had pawned the new kid off on me. The only advantage to me was that I was now no longer the "new guy." This quiet lad had no idea he was now enrolled in my course on "Get the News or Get Lost," and his teacher had a hangover.

I figured that the scary spinout at Field Circle had left a bump on Bob's nervous system because he was now making strange noises. His dark eyes stared at me as if he wanted to convey a message. Whatever it was, I thought, it had better be good. Losing the fire was not setting well with the man behind the wheel.

More funny noises came from the young man as he twitched in the seat. He was an Indian-looking fellow, with high cheekbones and a ruddy complexion. His face was fading from a Navajo tan to a light green. He opened his mouth, belched and then swallowed.

"Is there? Uh? Do you ever get used to these things? You know—fires and killings and things like that?" The question was punctuated with another belch.

The young man's inquiry and his uncomfortable condition made me pause. But I had no pity for him. Like a buzzard after road kill, I pounced on the moment. I jammed the little German's gas pedal to the floorboard. It responded like an ape on Ovaltine. Das Goot! Faking some excitement, I said, "I think I saw some black smoke over on Sylvester. Maybe that old lumber's got some new life in it."

I maybe shouldn't have spooked the kid, but a certain bit of meanness goes with a hangover. "Oh, fires and grocery store hijackings ain't much to stir your sperm. Just wait until you get your butt caught in a late spring tornado or get singed by a gas truck explosion. That's when you're ready for a blindfold and a cigarette," I said. The humor didn't register with the kid.

"Aw, the truth is you never know when you'll get caught in a blind alley with cops and robbers tradin' lead over your head. Bullets bustin' like bean farts. Happened to me once," I recalled, giving myself a rat-a-tat-tat drumroll on the steering wheel. Bob just kept looking greener and more glassy-eyed.

I was about to launch into another one of my "great escape" stories when the police dispatcher's voice cracked the silence of the cop's radio frequency with a growl: "510, the ME [medical examiner] is being sent over to 8812 Sylvester. DFD [Dallas Fire Department] likely found a 27 [dead person] at the location. You read, 510? Want to help out at 8812?"

An equally grouchy growl responded over the aging Monotone radio mounted on the hump of the Opel's floor. "Yeah, I'll meet 506 and the others at 8812. I heard 'em check out for traffic control." No. 510 was a police sergeant, a low-grade supervisor for the Northwest Dallas Patrol Division. He always sounded put out and disgruntled, with a thorny, condescending attitude.

For the most part, police didn't like fire duty. First, they had to direct traffic around the area. And too often, they had to do it standing in the middle of a hot, shadeless intersection with no hint of a breeze in the August air. This particular sergeant was known for giving news people a hard time. George Carter, a police reporter who presided like Judge Bean over the city pressroom, likened the old sergeant to some sort of malcontent with a cockle-burr up his butt.

In no time, the 510 came screaming up my tailpipe, lights flashing and siren howling. It nearly blew my little orange car off the road. I whipped that Opel off the old boulevard onto Lucas Street. The little German wasn't much for speed but was a corner-cutter deluxe. "On two wheels! How about that?" I bragged to my new partner.

Actually, the two-wheel maneuver was a bit too much for Bob. He was making noises again. "I don't guess we'd have a minute to pull over here and let me take care of something?" he asked. A loaded beer drinker begging for space in a long toilet line could not have been any more intense.

Now, in all honesty, I was known as a reporter with a cool demeanor, a thirty-five-year-old newsman with everlasting patience. Easygoing. But this was not the morning for Bob to lean on my good character qualities. Add to that the morning alarm clock that had clanged much too loudly and way too early. Bob's plea failed to reach me. I yelled, "No, I'm not gonna stop! No, you ain't gonna puke! And while I'm at it, no, I never get used to breaking in a new guy, and yes, we're going to be the last ones at this damned fire." I grabbed a breath. "And don't, for one minute, think you are gonna throw up in this car!" But it was too late.

The rolled-down windows provided a nice sweat-drying breeze. The rushing air also muted the sound of Bob's increasingly strange noises and carried off the awful odor from Bob ejecting his breakfast.

As I zigzagged around the potholes and patched places of orphaned, neglected Sylvester Street, I felt a twinge of guilt because my juices were flowing over the prospect of covering a fire death. Of course, I wasn't glad when someone died. But if someone had to leave this earth, now was the time and this was the place. Without flames or some other excitement, management folks back in the newsroom would not be pleased.

As I steered the news car into the fire area, over and above the Brut and other disgusting odors, I smelled something familiar. It was a distinctive smell, repulsively sweet, mingled with the odor of burning lumber. There was a burned corpse nearby.

Even though death was in the air, my attention had to be focused on the network of fire hoses lacing the street. Firemen don't give a damn who you are if you are in their way. They know you have a job to do, but don't run over their hoses. They have enough on their hands without fooling with a ruptured waterline. Missing a big three-inch line by that many inches, I sailed over the curb across a typical Dallas summer lawn, dry and ugly. The aging caretaker, an octogenarian armed with a rake and an attitude, was ready for a turf war.

"Off my lawn or I'll put enough holes in your tires, so it'll take a week to patch 'em," the yardman shouted. As I backed out of what was really just a field of weeds, I dodged all of the hoses by setting two wheels on the curb and the other two in the street. Then I felt behind the car seat to locate my camera and light meter. But just when it appeared that I was going to make it to safe territory, Mr. Police 510 strutted into view, lumbering from side to side like an eighteen-wheeler truck in a strong crosswind. The cop had caught part of the old man's yard act. He was twirling his nightstick above his head like a helicopter blade.

When I caught sight of him, I knew instantly it was "Sergeant Trouble." I took a deep breath. A near wreck, a sick colleague of doubtful use, a crazed yard-man and a fat man with a badge and a nightstick. It was just about enough to make a fellow forget that he had a hangover.

Ole 510 was actually an old acquaintance. I didn't like to recall our past association, but we had clashed sometime earlier when I was (according to him) an "overly aggressive" *Dallas Times Herald* police reporter.

Naturally, we recognized each other quickly. The old cop was also within earshot. "Don't ever let me catch you runnin' across somebody's lawn. And playin' leapfrog with them fire hoses." He continued, informing me that I was going to be the subject of a written police complaint.

With the voice of truculent authority, he added, "I know who you are, and you're on quite a few reports since you left the paper. You had a bunch of bad marks before you left the news rag, too. You are a capital smartass."

That did it! I'd had just about enough of the cop's nonsense. I yelled, "How about *shovin'* it?"

"Whad'ya just say, fella?" the sergeant snorted, charging a little closer. The nightstick continued to be a major prop in his theatrical display. "Ya better not get smart with me!"

I lost some of my nerve. "I said, 'Nice morning. Ya gotta love it.'" The cop knew what I had said but just grunted. Somewhere during the shouting match, Crowe had taken his leave. I was pleased. I was starting to take note that the kid was kinda gung-ho. That was a plus as far as I was concerned.

I hop-scotched and tiptoed over hoses, making my way to a far corner of the simple frame house. A ripple of flames still licked along the edge of the roof. There wasn't really much to shoot, but with the aid of the two-inch (telephoto) lens, a photographer can make a small flame look like a roaring inferno. Fully wound, the Bell & Howell can run off twenty feet of film. I cranked off something like fifteen feet. I already had my long shot establishing the scene. Now I just needed shots of firemen spraying water on the structure for cutaways. As usual, I was writing the story mentally as I shot it.

Then, before I could get back around the corner of the house, a stout stream of water shot across the remaining roof timbers. Hot cinders and water rained down on me, showering me with smoldering debris and peppering my three-day-old Robert Hall suit. I brushed fast, catching some embers before they singed the fabric. Unfortunately, the company insisted its newsmen wear suits and ties, even in the middle of August, no matter what story they were covering. I was not impressed with the policy. "Eleven whole bucks going up in smoke!"

Walking on the flattened hoses, I was making good time back to the unit when I heard a voice. "Hey, don't wear out our hoses with your dumb dance." The smart mouth was a new acquaintance I'd met when the fire department established a public relations office. Melvin Griggs was one of those guys who, if you lined up twelve men and told someone to pick the guy who was not a firefighter, you would pick him first. He had one of those Deputy Dog mugs that always presented a friendly front, no matter how dark a situation might be. Sort of a Pollyanna, but a real nice guy. Melvin told me that there was actually a pair of fire deaths in the house, not just one.

"Interesting," I commented noncommittally.

"Real interesting," Melvin said, adding, "especially when you take in consideration there is also a survivor."

"Huh? Holy cinders! Say that again!"

"Yep," Melvin confided. "You want the real drop on what went on out here, check in with that piece of flick over across the street—that female hunkered down on the curb."

Squinting into the sun, I focused in the direction Melvin indicated, shading my eyes to get a better look. There on the curb in front of 8812 Sylvester was a pale, blond figure of a woman coiled up like a pretzel. Hardly a woman—maybe more like a girl. She had her head buried in a pair of meatless white arms, crossed on her knees. Her dress covered everything but the essentials.

Trying not to pay too much attention to her condition and certainly not to her position, I made my way to her. She pulled her thin, flour sack print frock down to a more respectable position. Then I focused on her face.

"Would you talk to me?" I asked, in what I hoped was a benevolent manner. "I'd be much obliged to you if you could tell me in your own words just what went on around here. I'd get it right. Someone else might not understand your predicament, uh, your plight."

I caught myself. Those words were too big, too pompous. So I tried, "Somebody else might try to twist your words." I believed that this approach led a person to think a journalist of my caliber would be truthful, righteous and a straight shooter.

The young woman lifted her head off her knees. When the sunlight hit her in the face, she blinked like a barn owl as her chocolate-brown eyes adjusted to the strong midmorning rays. I thought maybe she had been crying. She probably had cause to. But I couldn't tell if she was smiling or smirking when she said, "Why should I talk to you? I'm havin' to go downtown with the fire feller over there. They want me to give them somethin' called a statement. I don't feel like tellin' over an' over again what I know."

"Well just answer me one thing then," I pleaded now, needing something, anything that would make a story. I tried my best country spin, "Those were your people who went down when the house went up in flames, weren't they? They're gone now, aren't they? Pardon me a little bit, but I'd be figuring that you'd feel kinda bad right now. Sorta' remorseful. Most folks might be shedding a few tears or maybe bawling their eyes out." I bore down. What could I lose now? "Where do I get off with you on this thing?"

She was now standing, and I couldn't help taking note of how tall she was. She had height but little flesh. Call the face plain. The fading, homemade-looking dress didn't do much for that broomstick figure. It once was accompanied by a belt, judging from the empty loops around the waist. In a patch of dirt between the curb and the street, she was tracing *x*'s and *o*'s with her brown oxfords, the kind of footwear that is ugly but functional. She answered, "Let's get one thing straight." Her voice cracked up an octave. "Yeah, I was staying here, but I can't say I was really livin'."

A couple of firemen stopped rolling up their hoses and looked over as the high-octave voice turned into a screech. A newsman from a competing station lingered in the area, his interest piqued.

The woman was yelling now. "I wasn't living. I was about to die. It was toad-tough. Damned toad-bad." Fascinated, I listened as she continued her tirade, "Yep, them's my folks. Least she's my mom. Was my mom. He was a sorry-assed stepdad. Couldn't keep his hands to himself. Hell no, I ain't sorry they's gone!" The louder she got, the more country she sounded. The diatribe made me want to do a little cussing myself. If I'd just had my Cinevoice sound camera, I could be getting all of this on sound film. The old Bell & Howell I was toting was one real workhorse, but for recording sound it was worthless as tits on a boar hog. I just knew this was award-winning stuff I was missing. Curses!

I continued with what I had at hand. Again, with my best country twang, I pitched another question: "Them there, those folks, they's gone now. But I see no remorse. No sorrow, no tears. Ya gotta know I figure that's a little strange, don't ya think?"

She stepped away from that patch of scratched dirt and into the middle of the street, where she stopped and pointed a bony finger with an unpainted, chipped nail right close to my nose. Now a "she-dragon" had come alive, and there was fire on her tongue. She continued her outrage: "Them's rats, and for them rats I ain't gonna bawl. I wouldn't cry a drop if their butt hairs was on fire!"

Then she got real rural. "They didn't treat me right. Mama bitched me out alla' time, and that he-somma' bitch, he couldn't keep his dirty hands offa' my parts. To hell with 'em! And to hell with you if you think I'm gonna cry just so you can take a few free pitchers!"

I was totally engrossed in her tirade, but I wasn't ready for the finale, the grand finish. It was a zinger. She put her hands on her hips and took a step in my direction. I retreated some to give her room for…something. That something was, "Now, if you got five bucks on, I might give you a few tears, if ya want. Then again if'n ya got a ten-spot in your wallet, I might roll around in that dirt over there and throw a kinda fit." I was shocked and also found her pitch a might expensive.

I gasped as I turned to my stunned competitor. "She's all yours, Mr. Folsom. She's totally yours. There ain't no telling what she'd do for $7.50 and a movie pass." I hopped the other curb, waited for a fire engine to pass and gave a final holler. "She might even show you the water heater carpet!" For the first time all day I felt like laughing.

On my way back to the news unit, a ladder truck slowed to let me pass. The radio dispatcher broke the silence of the late morning air. "Signal 11, Box 756. Out taps at 11:00 a.m." That made it official. The fire was over.

That day's fire story was most likely too late for the afternoon *Times Herald*. There was a small chance that the story could squeak into the financial edition that bedded down at 1:45 p.m. Newspaper editors disliked television news, primarily because it robbed them of their morning leads. What could have been a front-page lead had popped up on the 10:00 p.m. television news. Were they scooped? Maybe not, but news? Not anymore.

After a few snorts down at the Press Club, one editor at the *Dallas Morning News* confided, "When I see one of our front-page stories on the 10:00 p.m. news, I call down to page make-up and tell 'em to bury the story. Put it back near the classifieds if you have to." He said that it makes readers think television honchos don't know how to judge news.

The late morning air still supported that peculiar odor of burned wood and human flesh when I finally remembered Bob Crowe. Now where was the "boy"? Then I heard him laugh as he approached. I asked solicitously, "How're you feeling? You look like you're doin' a lot better. You got some color back in your cheeks."

Bob lowered his brows, "Yeah, I'm doing real fine. Just needed to get a real good, deep breath without whiffin' up that funny smell," he said. "By the way, I may have done better than I thought." He turned and headed around the front of the car.

"Yep," he continued, "I saw you were takin' care of the fire pictures, so I just thought I'd do some visiting. There was another cop over there on Hawthorn Avenue, directing traffic. Anyway, what he gave me was some pretty interesting stuff. It was just neighborhood gossip, but the cop said he'd heard that the girl may have had a big hand in what went on here today. Some had the notion she may have killed 'em and set the house on fire."

That kid looked me squarely in the eye, snapped his head in a knowing nod and closed his notebook with a strong, confident flip. I blinked. Bob cleared his throat. "Guess you get used to this kind of work after a while," he grinned.

I just inhaled deeply. I got trumped and we both knew it. A ho-hum story that reporters find routine is the kind of story you cannot get careless with. It will come back and bite you in the butt if you don't ask enough questions.

I tried to concentrate on what had transpired during the last couple of hours. Just another fire, a couple of deaths, an unpleasant survivor. She was a little abrasive, nothing too suspicious. But was she an arsonist? A murderer? Damn it!

I steered my news unit out of the fire area and toward Maple. "Dang it," I chastised myself for not coming up with that piece of information. I knew I had kissed off the story too early. Too many distractions, bad concentration. I sure didn't like to miss any of the facts.

Later, my little orange German was purring down Maple toward downtown. Some of the Maple scene was changing, becoming more eclectic. Older stretches of Maple sported buildings like the venerable Stoneleigh Hotel, but toward town the thoroughfare was getting a tad glitzy, especially down around Ross Avenue. But I liked to see changes in what was now becoming "my city." I was proud of the fact that there wasn't a spot in town I couldn't get to in a matter of minutes.

I instinctively headed for the Greyhound bus station on Commerce Street. From its aging art deco station, the Turnpike Express left on the hour for Fort Worth. It rarely left without a bag of film for WBAP, the cowtown station. All of its facilities for broadcasting were thirty miles to the west.

As I tossed my shipment to a sure-handed attendant, I was wishing I had a little more positive information about the fire. Maybe my new best friend Bob could come up with a few more facts at lunch that could substantiate what he got from the cop.

"Ya hungry?" I asked Bob as he bounced back into the car.

"I could put away a biscuit or two," Bob said, John Wayne style. Then, "I'm not an expert on teamwork, but I think we work petty good together. Make a fine pair of reporting partners. Whaddya think?"

Here I drew the line, new best friend or not. I figured that the kid was talking his way to a plateau not yet earned or ready to be bestowed. But I'd play along. "Yeah, we'd be okay. Might work out...if you'd quit puking in your shoes!"

"Well, you could have stopped. I wouldn't have thrown up on your car floor," Bob shot back. He feigned a gag and pitched his head forward toward the floorboard, grasping his throat, making a choking sound.

"Smart ass!" I forgot my New Year's resolution as I slammed the gas pedal to the floor. The car accelerated like a shot. Bob's head hit the semipadded dash.

"You are sick, man," Bob grinned as he checked his nose for blood. "If I'm gonna team with you, you oughta' sign up for some serious psychological attention," he snickered.

Free Press, Free Lunch?

The fire on Sylvester Street was tapped out at 11:00 a.m. Examining my singed, damp clothes, I reflected on the harm even a small fire can wreak on a newsman's new Robert Hall suit. Then I turned my attention to other matters.

Driving toward town, I ignored my partner, rookie Bob Crowe, while I caught the light on Ervay. Then back on Jackson, one-way westbound, careful not to wing a wino scurrying to a free lunch dished up at the Presbyterian Church Stewpot. No need for him to hurry. He wasn't late, just last in line.

A red light halted traffic at Akard Street. It was easy to take a right, but not just yet. One of the benefits of getting stopped at a downtown red light was the "stepping lively" parade, a daily treat for motorists, taking place right before their eyes. It was a good show, happening every morning, noon and evening as the office buildings spilled out some of the most fetching female office help in the Southwest. With high heels and tight blouses, the girls were, for the most part, dressed to the nines. Most of them surrendered their lunchtime to hurry to the stores and liberate racks of fashionable dresses at bargain prices. And Neiman Marcus, a couple of blocks east, tempted even the low-salaried. Titche-Goettinger was difficult for newcomers to pronounce but was no trouble to locate, just across from the police station. The ladies had to hurry to get over to A.

Harris or Sanger Brothers and back to their desks in time to scarf down a sandwich. But a really fast secretary could throw in a potty break, too.

Judging from the outpouring of female beauty from the AT&T building alone, "stepping lively" was a parade worth watching. The best viewing place was at the wind-whipped corner of Ervay and Main. Not only did the naughty wind lift skirts to an appealing height, but with that force, it also took two hands to return the hems to a level accepted by a Baptist deacon. If you were into this "sport," you could judge a woman by her ability to pin the flying skirt with her purse in one hand and a load of packages in the other. But the witness to this spectacle also had an obligation to not get caught watching and appear as though seeing nothing. That means wearing a nice Adams snap-brim hat, lowered to eye level, hiding the gaze.

The light slipped to caution and then green. I figured it was time for lunch. "We can still make the Kiwanis Club lunch deal here at the Baker Hotel," I told Bob. I whipped my slippery little sedan into the parking space on the west side of the hotel. It was marked off for taxis, but a news unit could rip off taxi space if it displayed a city police parking pass. In fact, a working press person with one of those parking passes could leave a vehicle just about anywhere there was a space.

"This club should have a good speaker today," I noted from the program. "Quick and simple." It was mailed to us down at the bureau. I saw it when I went through the file yesterday. They'll think we're coming to cover the program. We'll get a free plate of whatever it is that they're chowin' down on. Not a bad swap. Of course, if their story don't make air, it may be a while before we can sponge off 'em again."

As we took the elevator to the aging hotel's mezzanine, I thought about the string of free lunches I had put together not too long ago. For thirty-one working days, I scored on the lunch circuit, free. In the world of news gathering, that was probably a freebee record. It included noon dining at some six civic clubs, the nutty Boneheads group get-togethers and the tasty victuals that the athletic teams spread at the weekly news conferences. The Texans and the Cowboys really did treat with a tasty trough. Free beer was a great draw.

If all of the lunch faucets went dry, there was always Sheriff Bill Decker's ptomaine domain. It was good food for jail fare. News people were not only welcome to fork up food at the "Crossbar Café" but were also encouraged to sup at the convict quarters on the sixth floor of the Criminal Courts and Records Building there at Main and Houston. Decker would always say, "It ain't exactly free. Taxpayers foot the bill, but you're a taxpayer, aren't you?" What probably really lay behind all this camaraderie was a devious public relations plot. With each spoon of pinto beans, a journalist could see a plea for a bond issue for a new jail. Hitting the free lunch trail started out as a lark, but I soon found out that it was a good way to stretch a paycheck. Lord knows news wages were low enough.

Unfortunately, after a thirty-one-day string of free meals, there was a rude ending to the great freebee challenge: I got food poisoning. I went with a friend to scarf down a lunch at the Episcopal Hospital, where his wife worked. Usually chicken something, or something and chicken. Always a healthy salad. Never a bad free meal. But around midafternoon, my digestive system started to rebel, and it became evident that the city might not have enough restrooms. Actually, I didn't like to talk about it much. In fact, I was somewhat embarrassed about the whole venture, especially the place where I got the bug. A hospital certainly was the last place where you'd expect to get food poisoning.

Word of the collapse of my free spree swept through the city's journalist joints. The news community wasn't exactly stunned, but tongues did start to wag when word came in that my free lunch string was history.

At the Baker Hotel, we joined a couple of latecomers as they entered the big dining area. We wiggled between tables and chairs, making our way to the front of the room. The master of ceremonies read the details of the club's last project, but no one appeared to be listening. Their interest seemed to be on the food still being served.

I nudged Bob. "We're in luck—we eat. Follow me." We found a couple of vacant chairs right up close to the head table. I turned around in my seat, aimed my camera at the speaker and pushed the button. The camera made a picture-taking sound. The speaker looked right down the lens barrel and flashed his brightest smile as if to convey a message to those who weren't paying attention.

A waiter I knew from my many appearances on the luncheon circuit saw me come in, and within minutes we had plates before us. I inventoried the dish. Green peas with mashed potatoes, brown gravy and a rather meager offering of well-cooked roast beef. I had to make a lengthy grab across the table for the remaining roll, nice and hard on the outside and real soft in the middle. Those rolls were ideal for sopping up all of that gravy. A guy could actually get his fill just on that gravy and rolls.

The tinkling of table silver and restaurant china provided an accompaniment to the speaker, who was detailing the nuances between canoe safety and the standard propeller-driven craft. "Safety first, safety last and safety always," he emphasized, pounding lightly on the rostrum. I got up once or twice, pretending to take pictures.

Each time I returned to the table, though, I noticed awkward expressions on the diners' faces. Some sniffed as if smelling unpleasant odors. Some even covered their noses. Obviously, they smelled something bad.

One Kiwanian said something about "burning cardboard," and another, "wet lumber." I never looked up as I swallowed the remainder of a roll soaked in gravy. If Bob noticed anything, he never let on. Turning to the diner next to him, he asked, "You gonna finish that meat on your plate there under the potatoes? I'm kinda hungry. Breakfast just didn't stay with me very long."

Finally, I got up to "film" the closing remarks of the speaker, who sounded like he was about to run out of gas. He sputtered, "And gentlemen, when you crank up your boat motor, make certain the propeller is clear of hands, arms and your mother-in-law. Remember to secure your trailer hitch. You don't want it to come loose as you watch your boat passing you on a downhill grade." He laughed. Those in the audience who hadn't left the room, or started their afternoon nap early, clapped politely.

I returned to my seat, but my chair was not where I'd left it. It was against the wall, away from polite company and sensitive noses. I knew full well what had really happened. "Oh well, the Robert Hall fire suit didn't fit in here anyhow."

Later I did claim responsibility for the change that happened. Newsmen covering civic luncheons were pleasantly surprised to find that they had their very own table, always near the kitchen, labeled "PRESS."

The Press and the By-God FBI

N ews is the first draft of history." That declaration may be kinda dumb and naïve, but the words kept running through my mind as I refreshed myself at the little snack shop in the unusually quiet Dallas County Courts Building lobby.

As big and old as the courthouse was, it was still a pleasant place to escape from the blistering summer heat. I was enjoying one of my favorite midafternoon snacks of cold Royal Crown Cola and a tiny bag of tasty Tom's peanuts. It was sorta' like a mini-meal. It lasted longer when you poured the peanuts inside the large RC bottle. "Major!" I smacked my lips, using one of my favorite exclamations. I turned my head so no one would see me licking the salt off my lips. That salt was also part of the delight.

Upstairs, judges' gavels and prosecutors' mouths were silent. Summer continued to hold lawyers', bailiffs' and clerks' vacations hostage down on the breezy Gulf Coast or high up in the cool mountains of Colorado. During vacation time, there was little foot traffic from Main Street, past the pressroom and upstairs to the second floor, where Judge Henry King and Judge Frank Wilson dispensed justice. Mostly, bail bond runners' resoled shoes and female visitors to see their jailed boyfriends, their clopping heels echoing up and down the white marble steps.

For entertainment, a few representatives of the hall of justice's male population positioned themselves where they could eyeball some of the finest legs in the county. There was always a parade of secretaries up and down those stairs. Every now and then, some perky young stair climber, aware of the watching game, would flip a hem and show a thigh just for fun. I was never much of a leg man, but I might admit to a close friend that I was delighted by a nice-looking derriere.

From Main Street, almost dancing up the first set of steps, came Charlie Messmer, one of the law community's sharpest dressers, garbed that day in blue and white seersucker with a very expensive Panama hat. Nonchalantly, he sidled up to me and announced that there must be a bank robbery in the vicinity.

"There was a rather disturbed young man," Messmer said, "running down Main toward Lamar shouting something. Sounded like he was saying, 'Bank robbery! Bank robbery!' He zoomed along the sidewalk, shouting and running. Kinda like a squad car that lost its policeman. Paid not a hint of attention to traffic lights. All lights were GO, even the red ones." Charlie had the incident down pat, another colorful recollection. He continued, "He had a camera at arm's length over his head."

I was afraid to ask, but I did. "Did he look like an Indian? Was he a little green around the gills?" I had a suspicion it was a certain newsroom competitor.

"That's the fellow. He one of yours?" Messmer asked.

Bob Crowe was on the job but out of control. I uttered a mild obscenity through a mouthful of peanuts and a dribble of RC. "Stick this in the corner of the pop box," I said, extending my half-full bottle to Ira Munster, who ran the concession stand. I was not one to waste my favorite drink. As my mama would say, "Waste not, want not."

I slapped a "thank you" on Messmer's back and sprinted down the steps to Main, where the Opel waited for action like a silent sentinel. As usual, a parking ticket flapped on the windshield. The Dallas Police Department had an old, stone-faced motorcycle officer who put tickets on parked cars the instant the time expired. He would wait and wait in the scorching sun for a car to become a violator. SLAM! BANG! On went the ticket, press pass or not. He was earning his place in the spotlight. He wanted his moment of fame. And he would get it the night of the Police Appreciation Banquet. It was always Mr. Stone-face Cop marching up to a rostrum for his award for writing the most parking tickets. Must have been the only time during the year he smiled. Someone said it might be just stomach gas.

That windshield ticket flapped in the breeze as I shot a U-turn right there on Main Street. That agile little Opel could turn on a dime and give you a nickel in change. Full bore, the little orange charger was floored back east toward South Lamar and the Texas Bank. I didn't look for Crowe or a parking place. I figured Crowe was spinning out of control somewhere, but I would get this bank robbery story. So I whipped the Opel around on South Lamar and plunged down under the bank through its convenient basement entrance. Lots of spaces down there, maybe. And free, too. Good thinking!

I bailed out of the little news unit, grabbing the Bell & Howell from the apple crate in the back of the Opel. No time for the Fritzo light.

The elevator light indicated that the car was nearing the basement. I thought it was fortuitous that the elevator was nearing my level just when I needed it the most. The door opened, and my mouth did, too. I froze. The lone occupant of the bank's elevator was the robber I was chasing. I had come face to face with a real live bank robber. The robber had come face to face with a frozen photojournalist. His gun was leveled waist high—my waist! My film camera, also resting about waist high, was pointed at the bank robber. The gun was silent. The camera was rolling. While it was hard to tell what was going through the robber's mind, it was easy to tell what was whirling through my mind—my whole life, that's all.

I, who once dreamed of being a reporter for the *El Paso Times*, was going to die in the basement of a crummy bank—the least prestigious downtown bank! I had a fleeting thought that I should have stuck with truck driving or surveying or pumping gas at the largest Conoco station in New Mexico. One squeeze of that trigger, and the robber could put a bullet hole in a reporter. Such a huge orifice would let spill buckets of knowledge siphoned out of such auspicious institutions as New Mexico State and Abilene Christian College. And I thought of that wonderful six weeks at Texas Western University. Or was that the Juarez College of Carnal Knowledge? And, Lord, as the lead penetrates my head, don't let me lose my feeling for wonderful Southern Methodist University!

But reflections on my academic life in the Land of Enchantment and the Lone Star State needed to be left for a more opportune occasion. If this was going to be *it*, it might be a good time to repent for masquerading as a brilliant journalist. Despite my sometimes brash public persona, I had always believed that I faked being smart. Despite having a mantel full of awards, I never thought of myself as anything but a stubborn gatherer of news. Well, maybe a little bit of a con artist. Possibly now a dead con artist in a bank basement.

Both paralyzed, the bank robber and the petrified newsman played face-off with each other. Who would act first? Which one would blink? High drama! Then, for some inexplicable reason, I thought I should say something. All I could think of saying was, "How ya doin?" It sounded like a kitten.

Suddenly, the whole thing was over in the wink of an eye. Much to my surprise, fear flashed across the cash crook's face. He dropped his gun. He raised his hands. I blinked. I was the most dumfounded dunce in the dark basement. A bandit just gave up in front of my eyes!

"Okay, soldier, it's all over. Hit the ground." The command came from somewhere behind me. I heard the shout, but it wasn't until I turned around that I saw my backup force: officers in uniform, with shotguns, ready to have a blast. A few guys in suits had quietly and expertly entered the basement from a lobby entrance. The bandit saw them first. He didn't like the odds. That's what wrote "surrender" on his face from the time he opened the elevator door. But for one instant I thought I was about to add "Bank Robber Captor" as a chapter in the life that passed before my eyes.

"Okay, soldier." It was a familiar voice. It had been a while, but I had heard that voice before. I turned toward the sound. Yep, it was Wayne Bates. "Bates from THE BY-GOD FBI," he would say. He was one more of the lawmen who had never taken a liking to one of the area's finest newsmen. He let his feelings be known loud and clear. I was at the top of his most-unwanted list.

I well remembered the occasion that propelled me to FBI shame fame. Actually, I had really tried hard to get on the good side of the police, but every time, something happened. I had been editor of a tiny biweekly newspaper in Garland, Texas, when a robber hit the bank in the new shopping center. Police broadcast the license plate that a witness had given to officers. I copied the number from the police radio. Then, just for the hell of it, I called a friend at the license bureau. Like a good county employee, she had the name, address and car make in no time.

As luck would have it, the name that the county clerk attached to the car was listed in the phone book. I had gone too far to give up now. Besides, this was why news was fun. I dialed the number listed in the phone book. A voice, completely out of breath, answered, "Yes?"

I cut to the chase: "Is this the bank robber?"

"Who is this?" the timid and breathless voice stuttered. So I told the voice that I was a newspaper man. The voice did not deny he was the robber. At that moment, I heard a loud, banging sound accompanying the stuttering voice on the other end of the line. Then a shout, "FBI!" replaced the banging sounds. The stutterer, now all apologies, said, "I have to answer the door." More shouting, banging and pleading, A gruff voice shouted into the phone, "Who the hell is this…and don't hang up!"

"I'm the editor of the Garland newspaper," I said. "And who the hell are you with your bad phone manners?"

"If you need to know, this is Bates with the FBI. How the hell did you get on this line?"

I told the FBI that I had ways of acquiring information and that only a subpoena or a crowbar could pry the secret from my quivering, dry lips. I was, understandably, a little hesitant to tell the feds that whenever I wanted to, I could hear everything over the FBI radio frequency.

"You could have got us killed today, fellow," Bates barked, warning that as soon as the bank robbery business was taken care of, I—Mr. Newspaper Man—could expect a visit from "THE BY-GOD FBI." With that, it became more apparent that now one more law enforcement agency was not taking a liking to me. The list was getting long.

But back in the bank basement, it didn't take long for the wolf pack of news gatherers to surround me and the officers who now had the robber cuffed in the back seat of the federal sedan. All of the reporters and lens hawks wanted "my story," along with the FBI version. I was more than happy to comply. But then I really pissed off Bates when I asked the photographers if they wanted a shot of us together, shaking hands. Bad move. Bates muttered out the side of his mouth, "Now you've crossed the line, my idiot friend."

The strained silence that followed was broken by a familiar voice. "Way to go! I've got you on film all the way. I thought you were gonna get killed for sure." Bob Crowe was just a little bit excited. He swallowed a belch and came up with the quote of the day. "I'm crazy about covering bank robberies, aren't you?"

My thoughts were a little more hedonistic. I sure could use a cold Pearl beer. There was time to make a bus shipment of the film to Fort Worth. Thank god the terminal was close to the Press Club, where I had a tab. I thought I'd just let the RC and peanuts age.

A Very Scary Situation

The most misnamed piece of rolling stock in the Trinity Valley pulled out of the downtown Dallas bus station belching diesel smoke and creaking like a westbound stagecoach. The Turnpike Express worked its way along the turnpike to Fort Worth as usual, toting a valuable sack of film canisters with pictures for the 10:00 p.m. *Texas News*. The bus loped along like a jackrabbit through Grand Prairie, the womb for generations of mighty fighter planes. It was really blowing and going as it lumbered through Arlington, home of the General Motors assembly plant. It didn't stop until it reached its motor barn at Jones and Calhoun Streets in downtown Cowtown—hence the name "Express." It was the last nonstop bus of the day going that way. For Channel 5 newsmen in Dallas, it was the most important nonstop bus. Stories shot after sundown had to be hand-carried thirty miles to the west.

As I deposited my film on the last bus to Fort Worth, I made an illegal U-turn out of the Greyhound station on Jackson Street. I had a decision to make. I could go by my loft down by Fair Park and feed a hungry cat who probably wanted an ear scratch and tummy rub as much as a ration of those dry chunks that only dogs relish. Or I could stop off at the Jefferson Hotel for a very cold Pearl beer and a friendly, flirty word or two with Jackie, the saucy bartender who ran the dark watering hole called the Walnut Room. The Walnut Room won.

As I pulled into a no-parking zone, I pitched my parking pass onto the dashboard, which was cluttered with aging parking tickets. Actually, I felt a twinge of conscience. I had great affection for my cat, Duncan, WFC (World's Finest Cat). Duncan was probably my only true friend on this man-kick-dog planet. But I quickly dismissed any feeling of neglect. That cat was probably driving the mice crazy as they scurried here and there, shopping for their late-evening crumbs. Duncan was a pro at surprising them on their way back to their hole-in-the-wall homes.

At the Walnut Room, I flung the bar door open and light blasted the room. The two customers shaded their eyes to see who entered and then reestablished their strangleholds on their drinks, continuing in conversation and paying no attention to me. Jackie was washing glasses. With one hand she grabbed a Pearl from a box of chipped ice, ripped the lid off with a nearby Coca Cola opener and plopped it down on the countertop with a Budweiser coaster underneath. Without even looking up.

Now aware that I was not going to be officially recognized, I carried on by myself. "Well, howdy there, Mr. Shipp. How was your day? Any big news—killings, cuttings—anybody bleeding badly? We here in the Walnut Room have been so busy we can hardly find time to say howdy to one of our favorite customers."

I halted my soliloquy to take a big swig of the Pearl. I noted Jackie's glance and cockeyed smile. How could she not think I was funny, cute and just a half a degree off darlin'? Well, the truth was, I knew she didn't. Most girls didn't. Sometimes I thought it was my looks, my slightly crooked nose that sent once-willing women the other way. Anyhow, Jackie did her playing around with a criminal lawyer. There was an army of them around these parts since the courthouse was only a block away.

"Okay," Jackie said, shaking the water off her hands as she reached for the first of many towels that would be soiled before closing time. "What's the latest? Thrill me, chill me with news from the outside world."

I had a not very important, sobering story. "Well, I just did a story that's probably not worth the money it took to ship on the Turnpike Express. It's a sort of a sad little tale. It will never see the light of a news program." I didn't know why, but it disturbed me a little. I didn't want to shout, so I summoned Jackie up a little closer with a wiggling motion of my forefinger. As she bent over the counter, I couldn't help taking a quick peek at her ample bosom, generously exposed beneath a starched, peasant blouse.

"Got this 27, dead person call, from over on the good end of Reiger, just shortly before four this afternoon," I said. "There's this pretty little duplex with green shutters and a flower bed or two. Nice place. Only thing strange was that there were cop cars all over the place. Every officer who deals with bad-assed, killin' types crime was already there."

"The usual troop of news gatherers either hadn't appeared or hadn't heard the call on the police frequency. When I got to the door, a crime lab guy was going in. I just went in behind him. Over on the east side of the place was a bathroom with several detectives lookin,' pointin' and whisperin'. The subject of their conversation was a plump woman, naked as the day is long, wedged between the bathtub and the commode, with not a stitch on," I continued. "She was being given the once-over by a half-dozen men. One of the guys said he thought she was a Baptist minister's secretary, an old maid who looked like she'd had a heart attack after taking a bath."

"I backed off into another room and took a long shot, about twelve feet out of a twenty-foot wind on the Bell & Howell. Got pictures of the detectives standing in the hall talking and waiting for the medical examiner. They had been so occupied with their conversation that they didn't notice there was a newsman present until they heard the noise from my cranky old camera," I said. "One of the newer homicide detectives saw me. He raised his hand and motioned to me to get out. 'Another new, up-comin', chicken-shit rookie,' I thought. There were more of them than there were good guys. Not like in the old days, when I worked the police beat for the *Times Herald*."

"What the hell was the deal?" Jackie asked, now caught up in the yarn. "Sounds like it was what you guys call a no-story story. I've been around the block with you mugs. I know your lingo. Where's all this going? Ready for another really cold Pearl?" Of course I was. Especially out of that box with the iced-down bottles. Dang, they were cold.

"The point is this. That was a sweet lady. Said her prayers diligently every day. Never looked at the dirty words some kid chalked on the sidewalk. Always kept her skirt down so a nice-looking knee wouldn't give anyone a lewd thought. A man had probably never seen her with her clothes off. Just the mere thought of paradin' naked would have stopped her Christian heart," I continued. "I say all this to close with this one point: What a way to die. Buck-naked, exposed to the world with a half-dozen old hard-nosed guys with hairy legs gawking at her sinless body. How humiliating. She deserved better. What a crooked, unfair world. I'm gonna go home and feed the cat. Give me a beer t' haul out."

A few minutes later, I plopped myself down on the kinda cheap, thin Opel car seat. "Germans make a fine car but don't know nothin' about padding. Could be them Krauts had their own butt cushion built in," I thought as I scrunched down for more comfort. I took a long pull on my "take-out" Pearl and could see in the west what was turning out to be a prize sunset. I loved sunsets. Dawn was good, but when the sun flared and faded in the west with its campfire colors, it was more than wonderful.

When I reached my third-floor home in Fair Park, I cut the power to the Opel at a spot where I could keep an eye on the car. When I glanced up toward my quarters, I saw Sir Duncan, who was barely visible in the fading twilight, up on the roof, looking like royalty. He was there one second, then *poof*, he vanished in an instant. Then he would show up via circuitous routes through old building cracks leading to the door of "his" house.

"It's a wonder you didn't have the door open and dinner fixed," I said to my handsome tabby with the tortoise-shell design. He was a distinguished-looking fellow with a leonine face. And Duncan was one fast cat. He shot untouched through the crack as I opened the door. Oblivious to all the small talk I directed to him, he went straight to his dinner dish, apparently starving. A few morsels were left from his morning feeding. They weren't to his liking. He wheeled like a soldier doing a left-face, not happy.

Now weary, I plopped down on my aging couch to flip through a stack of what appeared to be worthless mail. Duncan dodged the flying envelopes sailing toward a wastebasket and leaped up to my lap. No invitation was needed. Attention was expected and taken for granted.

While Duncan got his ears rubbed and chin scratched, I turned my attention to the barnlike room, taking inventory of what it lacked. Some of my friends had gotten on my case for taking up residence in an old building across from Fair Park. I wasn't sure what a ghetto was, but I thought that maybe it meant that my location qualified as socially unacceptable.

Sometime in years to come, this third-story space would come to be known as a loft. But now it was a rather spartan place. Forty years ago, enterprising merchants bartered for a string of brick buildings here along Exposition and Haskell Avenues. That was when South Dallas was "the" place to live. The art deco buildings of the State Fair of Texas across the way did not seem to hurt the area. But then people started moving north. They left their stately mansions and the neighborhood deteriorated.

The building Duncan and I roamed around in was the project of an enterprising newsman, Slim Murray, who spent all his beer money on old buildings in less fortunate parts of downtown, like the Fair Park area. After getting his feet wet with a few individual buildings, he bought a whole street full of castoffs in a run-down, abandoned factory area. Friends told him it was a worthless stack of bricks. Slim did not waver as others laughed. Later, no one laughed when the "worthless pile of bricks" was transformed into the West End, one of the hottest tourist areas in Dallas. Slim talked me into occupying a piece of this old Fair Park area building that actually had living quarters of a sort. With some fixing and fudging, we more or less renovated a run-down old space on the third floor—a walk-up with no elevator. Duncan never complained. It came with mice and an occasional rat. Slim threw in an old, used toilet and an ancient four-legged tub. He also blessed me with a used refrigerator, or icebox as I still called it. An ancient kerosene stove was ready for winter duty, while an air-conditioning unit labored against the dreadful Dallas summer. It had seen many such seasons, and it continued to serve—*how* was a mystery.

It all came with the words, "It's yours practically free if you will just keep an eye on the property and pay the utilities." What a deal! I had heard of urban pioneers, and now I was one.

Once El Gato had been served his evening crunchies, I felt I had space for a snack to tide me over until morning. The old Kelvinator with the cooling unit perched on top always held a selection for a diner who was not too particular. This evening's dinner consisted of a hard-boiled egg, peeled and sliced. The wheels of egg were layered between two pieces of toast slathered with mayonnaise. A half-dozen out-of-date potato chips and a half-eaten dill pickle completed the meal. Luckily, one cold beer nested in the crisper. A half-pack of Salems provided a cigarette for dessert.

Duncan had a built-in clock that provided him a schedule as accurate as that of any trainmaster. It was bedtime. He had selected a spot on the end of the bed that was spread with a delicate, lavender-print sheet. In my family circumstances, living on the empty prairies of the West, a certain economy of living was developed. There were no bedspreads on the beds. In summer there were just sheets—pretty, colorful sheets. The sheet Duncan was now stretched out on was one of Sanger Brothers' best. In winter there was always a patchwork quilt, beautiful and colorful, lovingly stitched by a circle of churchwomen.

My bedtime rite was a male thing. In those early prairie years, when men readied for bed, they hung their pants on a chair or hook close to the bed, so they could extend an arm in the dark to easily find the trousers. For whatever reason, a fellow could be in those clothes and out the door in jig time. Today's photographer lore insisted that there was a hotshot photographer, John Gudjohnsen, who could get out the door in a minute forty-five. Others wondered if his forefathers from Iceland had anything to do with his dressing speed.

The Big Ben clock with luminous painted numbers displayed 2:00 a.m. when I was jolted awake to the ringing telephone echoing in my big, high-ceilinged room. Thick with sleep, I answered it. There was a fire down on Hatcher Street with at least one death. My immediate thought was that at least it was summer and not freezing. Anyway, fires didn't take too long to shoot, and Hatcher was just a beer can's throw to the other side of Fair Park. I swung my feet out of bed, and my legs were in my pants before my feet hit the floor.

On Hatcher, I found a parking spot in a vacant field just across from an apartment complex. By now, firemen had control of the blaze. All was routine except for the large crowd that had gathered. They were restless and noisy. A few were really angry. "And rightly they should be," I thought. I always felt bad when I had to film a story where people lost loved ones.

I thought I could make out an ambulance in the dark a few yards away. I shouted at the vehicle silhouetted against the lights along the freeway.

"That you, Junior?" The real, legal name of the ambulance driver was Big Tiny Little Junior.

Tiny, a huge black man, responded with a chuckle, "Yes sir. It's me. What'd you do to have to get up and out this time of night? What boss you teed off this week?"

"Aw heck, Junior," I matched his banter. "Ya don't have to piss off anyone when you are the last man on the totem pole. Last man hired gets shuttled to the Dallas bureau and put on nights—every night!"

Junior loved to laugh, but he wasn't laughing now. "Let me give you a little warning before you get too close up there where those folks make a crowd," Junior cautioned, just above a whisper. "They done lost a baby in that fire tonight, and they ain't happy. Seems they figured that if that had been a white baby, those white firemen would have tried harder to get to it. They are thinking that way, and they aren't too pleased about it." He added, "You might take it easy up there when you take pictures. There's been some drinking goin' on. They may take their troubles out on you. Be careful."

"Thanks, Junior. I probably can use that," I said, while taking a couple of long shots, working my way in closer. I got shots of firemen hosing down the remainder of a charred room. I didn't use much film on the sad little sheet-covered body in the backroom crib. There was a flame or two lingering back behind the complex. I squeezed off a dozen feet with the telephoto lens. That telephoto made those tiny, flickering flames look like a roaring inferno. Good stuff with those two-inchers! So it was back out front again. Now I needed a close-in crowd shot.

It doesn't take a college graduate to know that alcohol and camera lights often don't mix. I sensed that a good deal of imbibing had taken place. Some spectators now wanted their pictures taken. Others wanted to holler, let off steam. Getting nervous, I decided to take what I had and ease to the clearing. It was about time, too. Some unkind shouts were starting to dribble in from back in the crowd. Something about "white firemen" and "white photographers."

Suddenly, I realized that I was alone, the only one working. I wondered where the competition was. Channel 4 and Channel 8 must have been sleeping in. "We could have split the crowd," I thought. As it was, I had to deal with the scene alone.

Several dozen angry residents were too close and too loud for comfort. I almost ran back to the car. Junior, from the hood of no. 607, shouted what I already knew: "You in trouble!"

The crowd was just about even with the car when I shouted to them, "You want to be on television? Want your picture on the air?"

I turned on my light. "Back up a bit," I shouted. They did. "A bit more." The light was on, and they could not see me slip into the news unit. "Back up some more." Then I couldn't find the ignition keys. "Help me here, Junior!" I shouted, my voice now carrying a touch of terror. "Can you hit your siren? Or something…lights, maybe? Help me outta' here!"

I slammed the car door, noticing that, for once, I had left the keys in the ignition. At least it made for a quick start. The piston chamber exploded with the first spark. I hit the foot-feed, hard. As light as the car was, it stayed grounded and spun out and away. It whipped around a bit, producing a good cloud of dust. Thank God, Junior had hit his lights and siren, a real diversion at the right time. A great escape!

Second Avenue was empty as I took the shortest route home. I tried to think about what just happened. With a delayed touch of panic, my mind had trouble fixing on any one particular element of that scary incident.

A river of sweat trickled down between my eyes and down my nose. My upper lip was beaded with sweat. I was shaking like a dog trying to pass a peach pit. I had never had any trouble on this side of town before. Hell, I lived on this side of town. Was the crowd's hostility justified? What if the mob had caught up with me? Could a little bit of race history been written that night down on Hatcher Street? I shuddered. There had been other times when I had been a bit nervous. But tonight I was absolutely scared.

Back at the pad, Duncan never looked up. Not a whisker twitch. Not a blink. I crawled back on top of the Spring Maid sheet, moving the cat over a little to make a comfortable space for my feet. I felt like I was one lucky dude. Duncan was indifferent.

Staging the News?

As a former military ambulance driver, I liked to practice my skills. That's why I was racing through Oak Cliff's tricky, twisting thoroughfares in an attempt to beat ambulance no. 604 to the emergency dock behind Methodist Hospital. I was pleased with myself as I zipped off Zang Boulevard onto Colorado and took a chance with an amber light at Beckley Avenue. From there it was just a sprint down the hill into the parking and loading area behind the hospital, the big jewel in Oak Cliff's medical crown.

I jumped out and grabbed my picture-taking gear. It was an accepted practice for ambulance drivers to radio the dispatcher of their arrival a minute or two before they were actually at their destination. It made their run time look better. No. 604 had done just that. Now, with its siren silenced, the medical machine coasted to a position for a roll in reverse to the unloading dock.

"Hi, Speedy," ambulance driver Mike Hardwick shouted as he exited the cab and raced to open the rear doors.

"Nothin' to it this time of the mornin'," I said, positioning myself so the sun wouldn't wipe out my camera shot when the paramedics unloaded the victim in the shade shrouding the dock area. "Not much street traffic, plus lots of know-how, my friend," I bragged, backing out of his way.

I recorded all of the action as the ambulance crew brought the victim of a scaffold collapse to the treatment facilities, both orchestrated with ballet-like precision. I checked my Bell & Howell's footage counter. It indicated that I had only exposed fifteen feet of film from the time the ambulance appeared until it was unloaded. I needed several more shots to give the Fort Worth newsroom editors something to work with. I certainly didn't want them bringing a footage deficiency to my attention later in the day. What I needed were cutaways of the ambulance attendants and some film of the accident scene. I would be here a while.

Returning to the mobile unit, I realized that I had parked next to a wall beside a giant mulberry tree. The falling mulberries had changed the Opel's hood to a deep purple as berry juice on the orange paint job created a sickening combination. The arbor harbor also sported an aviary of fruit-loving birds. The feathered berry-pickers weren't just chewing and spitting the nasty seeds and gooey residue on everything below. They were also apparently feeling the effects of the berries as a volatile and turbulent laxative.

I fished an empty film can out of my back pocket. Then, with the proper expletive—"You no-good, low-lifed somma' bitches!"—I sent the can flying into the middle of the tree. Feathers and fruit rained right down on the space where I had launched my assault. The news unit, which had survived an Atlantic crossing without a scratch or a nick, was now sporting a palette of paint resembling a bird's speckled egg. Its owner did not fair well, either. I now had a purple-spotted suit coat to match. Another Robert Hall suit shot to…thunder.

I leaned up against the back of the car, really pissed. By now the ambulance crew had cleared the emergency entrance and hopped off the dock after completing paperwork. Noticing that I was really irritated, their concern—or at least their curiosity—was aroused. Whatever all my muttering meant, it was too good a show not to have an audience.

"You need any help?" Hardwick asked without too much sincerity. "We'll run get you some." Lyle Tores, the helper on no. 604, was sympathetic. "I think you need a cooler-offer." He displayed one of two bottles of soda pop he was swinging between the fingers on his left hand. "I got a couple a bottles of Pomac out of the cafeteria drink box. Mike didn't want his."

I took a deep breath, exhaled and grasped the already-open bottle, saying, "You might just have the gift of life in here." After a deep breath, I emptied the bottle. "You ambulance boys may have just saved another life."

I changed the subject, inquiring about another acquaintance: "Say, what's gonna happen to old Troy MacElroy? Ya know, the ambulance guy who killed his wife?"

"Don't know exactly," Lyle said with disappointment in his voice. "Poor son-of-a-bitch is a nut case, whatever happens. He blew away his pretty young wife thinking she was breakin' the ninth commandment with their church preacher." This was much more than I had heard around the pressrooms over the past few weeks. There hadn't been any explanation about why Troy had left his duty down at the ambulance headquarters on Industrial Boulevard and driven to their little Oak Cliff duplex on Ninth Street, just a few blocks west of Zang. Like a maniac, he snatched a shotgun from the window rack of his Ford pickup, galloped up to fling open an unlocked apartment door and blasted away at a figure in a housedress, seated on a couch. He emptied the twelve-gauge with a three-shot choke in it.

"What we learned later down at the ambulance barn," Lyle continued, "was he blew her away for nothing. What happened was that Toni, I think that's her name—'was' her name—was getting counselin' from her minister. Ya 'member how hotheaded old Troy was…about half nuts. Shoulda' been him that the preacher was shrinkin.'"

"Sorta' cuckoo, like most of us meat-wagon drivers. Get that way haulin' the dead and dying for a living," Mike broke in.

"But anyhow. Toni was secretly getting head help from her pastor so she could put up with her nutty husband. She really loved him and wanted to keep their marriage from goin' on the rocks. Well ole' Troy gets wind of these sessions she's having with the preacher," Lyle said. "And you know the rest of the story. Damned shame. The worst part is that Troy later found out the truth, and if you think he was kinda bananas before, they say he's really going ape-shit down there in that jail cell."

"Probably won't have any trouble getting off with an insanity plea now," I offered.

"Yeah," Mike said. "Hear tell his lawyer says Troy just sits in that cell and repeats over and over his wife's words—her last words. When he came busting through that duplex door, she said, 'Hi, Honey, what a wonderful surprise!'"

He shook his head as he tilted the empty Pomac bottle skyward to determine if there might be a drop of the tasty nectar left. "Ya know, y'all are livin' under a dark cloud," I said. "The ambulance corps is getting the reputation of being a bunch of heathen renegades. Especially when that deal came out about you-know-who."

"Yeah, we may never live down what you-know-who did," Lyle added. "My mom told me to get another job, even if I had to work haulin' garbage. That was after she heard that one of our ambulance guys got in big trouble for feeling up a woman patient. She was talkin' 'bout that woman that was hauled to St. Paul Hospital with a heart attack and got messed with by the ambulance people. Mom liked to have had one of those attacks herself," Lyle said, using his index finger to quell a trickle of snuff juice escaping down the corner of his fast-moving mouth. "I was off-duty a few days when the word got out. Now, get this. She thought it might have been me! She said she figured it might have something to do with some of my father's sorry-assed blood in me."

"Whoa, ho," Mike said. "That's a black mark on us that's gonna be hard to erase. So bad that we don't even mention the name of ole what's-his-name. No way that's really us. Can't imagine what that woman was thinking as she was fightin' off a heart attack in the back of that wagon. Geeze! What an animal! Glad she lived to tell on the bastard."

"Well, all this Sunday school talk is makin' me thirsty again," I interrupted. "That Pomac ain't too bad. If they could find a way to shoot up every bottle with a little whiskey, they might sell barrels of it."

Then, remembering that I needed some more footage for the story, I asked Mike and Lyle to jump out of the ambulance again while Mike was closer and at a different angle. Then I reversed my position and shot from inside the ambulance. Staged shots? Not really. It made the story better. After the Methodist Hospital shots, it didn't take long to get pictures of the broken scaffold in far south Oak Cliff, where the accident occurred.

After tossing the film onto the Turnpike Express for Fort Worth, I phoned the Dallas Bureau in the county courthouse pressroom. A murder trial was about to wrap up in District Judge Henry King's criminal court. I processed all of this new information and then explained to Bureau Chief Jimmy Ford that I was short of film. Only had one can left.

"Better short shoot 'cause that's the last roll in Dallas until we get what's coming back from Cowtown this afternoon," Jimmy said. I made my way up the county courthouse's marble stairs, taking two at a time to King's courtroom, where the trial was in recess.

There I caught Will Alexander's attention. The assistant district attorney turned around. "Wait 'til I get through here and I'll have a drink with ya. But we're just about to sum up, and you don't want to miss my 'ride ole Sparky' closing. [The electric chair was called Sparky.] I'm gonna blow old Joe McNicholas clear out of his shorts."

I told Alexander that there was only one roll of film to record his "great closing," and that was only three minutes of exposure time.

"Hell, that's plenty. I'll just nod to you when I get ready to unload the good stuff," Will said.

I had to remind him of the rules. "You forgot I've got to get McNicholas's defense argument, too. Otherwise, I ain't givin' him a fair shake."

McNicholas, the court-appointed attorney for the accused rapist-killer, was rounding the corner from the hallway and caught his name. "Somebody announce the top five best defense attorneys in the Southwest?" Joe asked, squinting through glasses as thick as pop-bottle bottoms.

"Naw, Joe." Will was ready with a line. "We were just speculating how many times your poor eyesight led you into the ladies' bathroom by mistake. Wondered if you got a good peek before you played that 'Excuse me—my eyes, ya know' card?"

"You are without shame, Will," Joe said. "But I did see your mother there drop a couple of rolls of toilet paper into her purse. Guess she was planning to wipe a few tears when she's overcome by your closing."

"Hey, you jokers. There is not a road out of town that you could take that comedy on. Bad, bad stuff," I said, feeling like I had to add something to the discussion. The two legal eagles understood my dilemma and agreed to abide by my guidelines. McNicholas said that he would nod when he was ready for his minute and a half of fame. Alexander said that he would change his nod to a wink. "Be sure to speak up," I cautioned. I'll get good sound that way."

I looked toward the bench to see Judge King beckoning toward me. I approached. "What are you up to, son?" the judge asked, well acquainted with who I was. I told him of my dilemma and the arrangement. Judge King nodded his approval.

Staging the news? Set up or not, the filming of the arguments went off with precision. Alexander started his closing address very slowly, and then with a wink, he turned on a tirade. He didn't beg the all-male jury to send the defendant to the "chair." He demanded it.

Joe McNicholas had as much chance of saving his client's life as a coyote had escaping a trap. When it came time for Joe to plead before the panel of anxious jurors, he nodded as he began and quit the second the film ran out a minute and a half later. He really had no defense. He just asked the jury not to send the family breadwinner to the "great beyond." As the final arguments ended, I heard the film slip off the end of the roll.

In almost the time it took me to break down my camera equipment and pack away the sound gear, the jury elected a foreman and took a vote, coming back with a guilty verdict.

As I walked past the judge's quarters on my way out, I acknowledged His Honor with, "It don't take long when you know what you're doing, does it, Judge?" The judge responded, "Well, I've heard of those who attempt to fix juries, but I can't say's I have ever seen anyone fix lawyers."

"Just like Hollywood, Your Honor. Thanks. I owe you one." I addressed His Honor as I left the courtroom swinging an empty camera.

When I got to my car, I found a new parking ticket on the windshield of the orange Opel. But I was thinking about these things as I made an illegal turn onto Main Street. I decided not to concern myself with the fact that I'd set up the closings. Newspaper photographers staged shots all the time. "Stand here." "Show me the gun." "Salute the flag." There are all sorts of situations where adjustments have to be made to correct the composition—just makes for a better picture. Why wouldn't newsreel photographers do it? The main objection of the critics is that "it's not natural." They think that the first time an event happens is the only time.

If a motion picture photographer misses the initial action needed to tell the story, he is not, like print media, able to fall back on words. He has to have pictures. So, I thought, if repeating the action doesn't disturb the exact circumstance of the previous situation, it's okay.

Later that evening, my thoughts came home to roost like a pigeon on a mission. I had to work a double shift because the new guy, Bob

Crowe, called in with some excusable absence. That kid learned real quick. Whatever the circumstances, I found myself at a warring Balch Springs City Council meeting. As members threatened to do harm to one another, I slipped out of the combat zone just to check the goings-on with the Dallas police dispatcher.

I had learned a small trick about contacting the dispatcher. I'd put a dime in the pay phone slot. When the operator answered, I would say, "This is 697 calling 531." This meant to the operator that the police officer with badge 697 wanted to speak with the person at police dispatch extension 531. Once the connection was made, the caller got his dime back and had immediate access to the police dispatcher. While I was fishing the coin return for my dime, the dispatcher told me she was "Eaton." I matched her with my 697. This dispatcher knew that was really a reporter's call number, not a police person's. She responded as I wanted: "Body in the Trinity there off East Colorado Boulevard."

Figuring that Oak Cliff had a more compelling story than the fighting city council of Balch Springs, I tried to figure out how to get to the drowning as fast as I could, knowing that I might be behind the body recovery. I spun off Hawn Freeway onto Loop 12, hoping that the cops were taking care of other business and not looking for speeders. I knew if I was caught speeding it was another ticket for sure. I was certain that I was on some sort of invisible police "get him" list. I was being stopped an awful lot lately. Most of the time the bulls let news people go. "Just doing your job, we know," was the sort of professional courtesy thing that I always expected would prevail.

Leaving the loop behind, I sped north on Zang Boulevard toward Colorado. From the moment I left Colorado Boulevard to climb in second gear over the Trinity levee, I could smell that nasty, muddy river that a generation of citizens wanted to beautify. Even with the lights of the city in my face, I could make out signs of activity on the riverbank. Maybe I wasn't too late. All things considered, though, signs weren't in my favor.

I followed the bent grass trail made by other vehicles to the river's edge. As I pulled up next to the ambulance, I could make out that it was no. 604, a good sign. It was my good buddies from the Methodist run earlier in the day. But there were no other television news units in sight. That meant that they hadn't arrived yet or (I didn't want to even consider this) that they had come and gone.

Mike Hardwick was about to mount the ambulance driver's seat as I rolled to a stop. "Naw, we ain't got no mo Pomac, Mr. Shipp."

"That doesn't matter." I was real nervous now. "Thank goodness you're still here with your load."

"Goodness ain't gonna help you, my friend. Your competitors done come, shot and gone," Mike said. He knew he had me between stink and stunk. "If Mr. Television News doesn't have pictures of that dead man, the smell of his predicament might get a tad pungent. Sorta' like the aroma emitted by the subject in question. That about right?" He was just having a little fun, and we both knew it.

"Okay, Mr. Hardwick, y'all have stroked your morbid sense of humor. You know what I need. Help me out with a body picture. Please."

Mike told me that they'd been marked out too long now but agreed to redo the deed if I would, this time, remember the favor. "I still remember that time you showed a shot of us dropping a body that we were unloading over at Parkland. We promised everything but our firstborn if you would not show them shots. Ya did anyhow. Remember?" Mike recalled as he pointed his assistant to get the other side of the gurney.

Having done the drill a hundred times, the ambulance pair had the body in the water almost before I was ready with, "I'm rolling."

My Fritzo was flooding the scene with great picture-taking light. But when I said, "Let's go, boys," instead of recording a smooth "take out," I found my camera following a body that was starting to float downstream. To say the least, I was not getting the picture I wanted.

Everyone screamed at once. "Somebody get it…damn it!" The slick ground, wet from the first recovery, contributed to the loss of footing and our loose grips. There was a lot of cussin'. The body had taken on a life of its own.

Everyone was yelling. No one was thinking. I knew with certainty that if something was going to be done, I'd have to do it, because in the back of my mind I could see, not my station, but the other ten o'clock newscasts, announcing, "Body recovered from the Trinity tonight." Such a thing was intolerable.

Now past thinking, I dumped my camera and light on the ground and threw my body in the water. The Trinity River is about as nasty a waterway as you will find. Dallas dumps its sewage, treated as it may be, so Houston will have water to go with its bourbon. Right now it was difficult to determine which smelled worse, the river or the dead man it had claimed. Luckily, my feet found footing on a sandbar, which kept me and my decomposing companion from floating too far from help. With the lifeless man in my arms, I yelled at the two stunned attendants on the bank, "If you think I'm givin' this wino mouth-to-mouth, you better demonstrate first!"

Once the corpse was resting comfortably back in no. 604, we vowed never to recall the bizarre episode in polite society. "Might damage the reputation of us upstanding ambulance people," Mike remarked, with a small measure of pride. "And you, Mr. Newsman—your industry couldn't stand many numb-nut capers like you thought up tonight."

Later, I found a pair of old jeans behind the apple crate in the rear of the Opel. The change from the wet Robert Hall suit didn't eliminate, or even reduce, the smell of the river, so I made the speedy trip to Fort Worth with all windows wide open. Even with that, I could still detect odor de la dead man. But I took comfort in knowing that I got the pictures, even if I had to restage the scene a little. I'd often had to do that, always to improve a picture story. Why not? After all, it really did happen that way. Mostly.

A Sad Tale from East Texas

WBAP-TV Channel 5's ten o'clock newscast was called *The Texas News*. That label was always a question in the back of my mind. Why *The Texas News*? The TV screen would whirl with a montage of news pictures from here, there and everywhere. But the stories and scenes were nearly all from North Texas. A catchy little jingle signaled that it was time for the news. A round-sounding, mellow voice told the viewer that a loyal local merchant was picking up the tab for *The Texas News* at ten o'clock. It was a good buy because this was the most-watched newscast in the area.

More than likely, though, all of the stories would be from around North Texas: local banks being robbed, Mesquite City Council disputes, a three-legged dog climbing trees in Fort Worth and skinny models strutting the latest fashions from Dallas's Sanger Harris. All hometown, homegrown yarns. No statewide stories. So why the really expansive name? I found the answer in a story from Brownsboro.

It was one of those steamy July afternoons. I was enjoying the refrigerated air forced from the county pressroom's ancient cooling unit. But after a while, we reporters became aware of an unusual smell wafting through the room. Alex Madison, a news bum, was a lost, loveable Englishman who lived out of whatever wasn't occupied, mainly his deteriorating station wagon. While chasing stories on a freelance basis for Channel 5, he kept his foodstuffs in a tiny compartment in one end of the cooling apparatus. On this particular day, the unpleasantness arose when Alex's refrigerated grapes deteriorated, along with the bologna on his wilted tomato and lettuce salad.

"Alex! Where's Alex?" One of the reporters cringed as his nostrils sucked up the disturbing odor. Two giant Emerson ceiling fans stirred the ingredients to barnyard standards. But I was oblivious to the shouts, smell and stale air. I was just enjoying the product of the cooling machine. I considered refrigerated air the greatest invention of the twentieth century.

I was about to doze off when one of a half-dozen phones clanged like fire engines in a box canyon. I answered. My Fort Worth office told me to locate Brownsboro on the map. "Somewhere out of Athens in Henderson County," said Cody Veston, the Fort Worth news manager. "Big killing down there last night at a school board meeting. One or more shot dead. At least one laid-low but alive in the hospital there."

Happened last night? Why are we just now getting jacked up? And it's kinda far—hundred miles or so. I pondered these issues, and I still didn't know how I was going to get down there and back in time for a 10:00 p.m. news story. "Thanks. Thanks a lot." I was unenthusiastic. Dang, I hated to leave that refrigerated air.

I knew where Athens was. It was kinda like Palestine and Paris and Italy, all those Texas towns that had faraway sounds but were actually Lone Star places. Didn't even have to cross an ocean to get to Moscow. New London was not far from Brownsboro. But thinkin' wasn't movin', so I thought I'd better get hauling.

I cut south on Highway 175 and floor-boarded the Opel. I needed speed to cut the time, but mostly I needed the swift rush of circulating air to furnish cooling of some sort. I was a couple of minutes out of Athens when I saw a Channel 4 news wagon racing toward me—a competitor. The Channel 4 guy recognized me in the little orange gas-saver. He motioned to me, pulled over and stopped.

It was Joe Dave Scott. We had worked for the Abilene paper when Joe Dave was interning at SMU. At the end of the summer, he talked me into returning with him to Dallas. That was six years ago. "What the hell are you doing down in these woods?" Scott inquired, knowing that I was en route to Brownsboro. Already pissed that I was running late, now I got a new mad on realizing that the competition had done its business and was actually going to make the 6:00 p.m. news!

But we were friends, so Joe Dave spared me any ribbing and even passed along some advice. "Those Brownsboro people were not real happy to see us big city folks coming down here. They think we're sticking our noses in their business, especially right now when the business is tainted with the stench of killin'. I'd be awful careful down there."

Joe Dave's buglike eyes reflected a real concern. In as serious a statement as he could give, he added, "They told me I might ought to get my little pointed nose for news and my skinny ass back to Dallas or they would stick it where the sun don't shine." He told me it might be wise to heed their advice. "You might oughta mind what I say. This ain't civilized territory like our old Abilene." I said thanks; I'd ponder the advice as I looked for a place to turn around. Both of us knew I wasn't going to turn around. Now I was really curious. Besides, I liked a challenge. It varied the routine. It broke the monotony. I intended to meet the conflict (if there was one) head-on. I did appreciate Joe Dave's caution, though.

"Don't say I didn't warn ya," Joe Dave shouted as he rolled up the window on his new, air-conditioned Chevrolet news unit.

Before I geared up to go, I left the shift in neutral while I did some thinking. As I collected my thoughts, I popped open the glove box and felt around until I found an old cigar I'd ditched there months ago. Somebody must have had a baby. It must have been a girl—it was not an expensive cigar. I lit it and worked up a nice chewy wad, testing the product as I eased out the clutch and let the first gear whine on takeoff. By the time I was up to second gear, my necktie came off. My sleeves were rolled up as I made the shift to high. The Robert Hall suit coat was tossed on the floor of the back seat, where the camera and other filming paraphernalia were sorta' hidden.

Brownsboro was what city folks in that day and time called a burg. A municipal vagrant. No visible means of support—a tiny store, a small post office, a little of this and not much of that. If there was any action going on about the village, it was in front of the tiny, run-down store. There was movement there, on a sturdy, unpainted bench. Whittlin'. Three guys, three knives, three pieces of pine and one pile of shavings. I slowly pulled up as close to the front of the place as I could, but not so close as to block the bench occupants' view of the street. I was careful to leave the car very slowly, with extra caution. Nothing in that town looked as though it was done fast. I was not about to put a ripple on their pond.

I was even careful not to scare a circle of sparrows dancing around a handful of seeds spilled near an aging plank walk. I nodded a "howdy" to the bench fellows. One was whittling on what was left of a small two-by-two. One was admiring something he had reduced to almost nothing. A toothpick? And the other old boy was retooling, sharpening his blade on a pocket-sized whetstone.

The bench looked pretty steady, so I settled my rump on the far end. It didn't feel splintery, but it was begging for a new coat of paint. Probably was last touched up when the man sharpening his knife ordered the whetstone from Sears Roebuck back in the '40s. Anyhow, it felt good to get out of the Opel. A sudden breeze blessed the hot afternoon air and scattered the seeds that the birds were devouring. The sparrows were on their toes in quick pursuit, hopping and pecking to avoid losing a single grain.

The woodcutters' eyes were fastened on me. I was about to get psyched out by their stares. It was time to cut the tension. I eased a handkerchief out of my back pocket, wiped my brow and broke the silence. "Think summer'll ever get here?" I twanged with a joke twist to it. Without hesitation, the knife sharpener cleared his throat with a hock. "Don't rightly know, but we's about due for a blue norther, maybe tonight." The whole bench shook with silent humor. The whittler also cracked a Mona Lisa kind of smile.

"Not much going on down in these parts nowadays?" I drawled, with sort of a question mark at the end. I gave myself a ten-count as I waited for reaction to my baited remark. At the silent count of nine, the youngest, the one with the overall bib hanging at half-mast, popped up, "Ya shoulda' been around cheer last night. You'd a thought World War III broke out."

There was a knowing chuckle from each of the trio as their wrinkled faces rippled with humor. The bench shook again.

I counted to ten again. Then slowly, as if disinterested, I said, "How's that?" Suddenly, before I could unfold my mental notebook, all three of them were telling their versions of what went on at the Brownsboro Independent School District trustees' meeting the night before.

Mostly, they were telling about the shooting. What started it, who were the shooters and who got shot. These silent sentinels of Brownsboro's Main Street had held it in too long. They had to tell someone. They were telling one another the goings-on as much as informing me. They corrected one another and agreed on as much as they disputed the events.

They were still jawboning when I had as many facts as I could cram into my brain cells, wishing I had my notebook or a hidden tape recorder. The trio hardly heard my "much obliged" as I left the bench and headed for the car and the scene of all this crime. As I opened the car door, the sparrows scattered in a whirlwind of feathers, only to return almost before I closed the door.

Small towns are convenient. Nothing's far away. Finding the school building took no time. Other than a couple of church buildings, the school complex was the most prominent structure in town. Maybe the newest. Instead of taking advantage of the vacant parking lot in front of the structure, I chose a spot behind the building. An orange car full of camera equipment would attract attention like a barn fire. Thinking that the building was locked, I looked through the windows. Without much effort, I found myself staring at a large room with a long table. Papers were scattered about. A pair of glasses was abandoned in the middle of the table. I couldn't tell in the darkened room, but there appeared to be stains here and there about the floor. Blood? It was time for a closer look.

I located a big double door toward the south end of the school building. This door might have been used to drive large equipment like tractors in and out of a mechanical area. This part of the school building looked like an agricultural shop. In a rural area, the agriculture shop with its work area was probably the most important part of the building. This one was well supplied. It was secured with a board across the door, keeping it from opening. A fair-sized tree branch nearby flipped the two-by-four up from its moorings. As the door swung open, I was startled to hear a compliment and a question from somewhere behind me.

"Hi, good-lookin'. What's cookin'? Huntin' firewood?" The question came in a familiar nasal twang. I didn't even have to turn around to recognize Sue Connally way out here. Sue was the school or education reporter for the *Dallas Morning News*. In earlier times, I had been in her company a great deal, especially when I was assigned the school beat at the *Dallas Times Herald*. She journalistically kicked and whipped my butt six ways from Sunday when we first went head to head on the school beat. She charmed the male members of the Dallas School Board, and they cut her in on all the big news to come out of the district. Being merely male, I got cut out. But that was another time and another place. She was still with the *News*, and I had a television assignment to finish.

"Suzie! Scare a fellow into tomorrow, why don't ya? What in the name of the Dallas Snooze are you doing in a place like this?"

With that air of confidence that she usually exhibited, she abandoned the "cooking and good-lookin" bit and got down to business. No more "Ms. Friendly" as she said that she may have been the only one in the newsroom who knew where Brownsboro was. She was raised in Athens. Then she cut to the chase. "What have you found out?" I told her about the encounter downtown and the story I heard from the three wise men in overalls.

"Oh good, you can be of great value, just like in Houston," Sue cracked with a smile angling to the corner of her cheek. Then I remembered the time that I filed her story from the Texas Education Convention one night in Houston, while Ms. Morning News was being entertained elsewhere.

"When do you think you'll return all these favors?" I came on rather suggestively, stooping a little to look into her eyes. I fluttered my eyes a bit.

"You couldn't handle my paybacks." She pursed her valentine-shaped lips and made a kissing motion as she blinked her eyes. She followed me through the entrance of the garage area after I had flipped the bar off the big door. Moving through the agricultural shop, we focused on the adjoining hallway. The next lighted area was where war had broken out the night before. Those stains I had noted from the outside were indeed blood. With the wide-angle lens, I got my long shot from the end of the room. Then, with a fresh wind on the tired old spring of the aging Bell & Howell camera, and the one-inch lens in place, I photographed the pair of glasses with cracked lens and a bent earpiece lying on one end of the table. Finally, I placed some spent cartridges, which lay hidden in dark places around the room, on the table.

The two-inch telephoto lens brought the dried bloodstains into sharp focus. "I sure could use my Fritzo light," I said to Sue, who was now busy going through some papers she found scattered in the hall.

"Sure could use a photographer with a still camera," she said.

That's her, I thought; she came without a photographer. Interesting. On the other hand, she wouldn't have needed a photographer if I hadn't burglarized my way into the building.

Suddenly I remembered what the whittlers had said earlier. There was one board member so shot up that it wasn't advisable to take him any farther than the local clinic. A clinic in this burg? And hadn't Cody in the Fort Worth studio mentioned that somebody was shot but alive?

Now I was in a hurry to ditch Sue and see for myself. "Well, that's about it around here, I guess," I suggested. "I got to get on the road or I will never get to Fort Worth by news time." I wanted to escape having to tell her that there was a victim of the fracas not yet dead or being held in the county jail.

Now it was time to see if there really was a clinic in this one-horse town. Around the corner, sure enough, there was a little white structure with a neon sign that advertised "CLINIC" in large, purple cursive letters. It was highly visible in the faint glow of the dying sun that was smothering the East Texas woods.

I needed a plan to get access to whoever I needed inside that building. I pushed on a glass door opening directly into a lobby with that medicine smell like every hospital I had ever been in. I knew I wouldn't lie about anything. I never lied. I believed that truth and reality were the hallmarks of news gathering. A good reporter might just as well have "truth forever" tattooed on his forehead.

I had my camera tucked inside my Robert Hall coat, which I had loosely tossed across my shoulder. If I turned my right side toward the desk, the hump might not be so evident. A stout woman in a starched white nurse's uniform looked up from her recordkeeping long enough to inquire, "What can I do fer ya?" Had she been the slightest bit observant, she would have noticed the camera that made me look like the Hunchback of Notre Dame. I answered her question with real sympathy.

"I hear the poor old guy that got shot over at the schoolhouse last night might be wantin' to see some of his kin afore he passes. I'm here to see him." No lie there!

Still seated and more interested in her record book than she was in the implication of my statement, the nurse motioned to me to "go down this here hall to the third door on the right. Find 'im right thar."

58

"Much obliged," I responded in my very best Big Thicket twang. "I love those East Texas dialects," I thought. I allowed myself a moment of silent mirth. Actually, I was running over with glee. "That was the best. It was a major move! If this works out, it'll make a great yarn for the Joe Banks lunch bunch. Heck, it'll run the table!"

The door to room 103 was slightly ajar. It opened without a sound. A slightly built woman wearing one of those nonwrinkling print dresses had positioned herself across the dark room in a straight-back chair. Her head was cradled in her cupped hands. She raised her head as I entered, her sad eyes boring a hole in my face.

She looked plum worn out. The light from the flickering fluorescent overhead threw her features into sharp relief. I could see dark circles under her eyes. I expected her to say something angry or maybe threatening, but she looked dazed, as if in a trance. Against the opposite wall of the small room was a regulation hospital bed with the patient resting on his back. A hanging bottle with tubes running in and out of every orifice was sad evidence of his injuries.

I took quick advantage of any moment of shock or surprise that may have accompanied my presence in the room. "Hello, ma'm," I said, neighborly, "Heard about the awful thing that happened to your man there. I'm from far away, from Fort Worth." (How dumb was that introduction?) I continued, "We want to tell the truth about what happened down here. Really, the television station I'm with is connected with NBC out of New York City. Your story may make it all over the nation." I was talking, not really thinking, but something out of my mouth was keeping me in that room. I didn't really mean to play the New York card. It just slipped out.

"I can tell you've been praying over your man a lot today, haven't you?" I said, still surprised by my continuing success. I kept on. "I guess when you pray to the Heavenly Father, you are usually over here by your man's side. There at the bedside?" I asked, calculating a move to get the woman with the man in the same shot. A little communicating with the man upstairs would be a bonus. After she nodded in the affirmative to my suggestions, I assisted the woman up from her chair. I took her by her thin but firm arm. It had the feel of a working woman's arm, probably a farm woman. For some reason, she followed my every move and suggestion. There she was, seated by her man with her kitchen-worn hands resting on the mattress, her fingers forming a prayer-like steeple. I could hear her utterances but not the context. It could have been the Lord's Prayer or the Twenty-third Psalm or maybe just talkin' to the Lord.

The Bell & Howell clattered and clanked away. The scene was picture perfect, but on silent film. "Boy, what I wouldn't give for a Cinevoice sound camera right now," I thought. But really, the delicate light glistening off the lifesaving tubes and the grieving woman in silhouette making a deal with God told a story of its own. No words were needed.

Later, the darkness had softened the heat of the torrid day. As the news unit flew through the night toward Fort Worth, the wind was rushing over me from every window. The night was still warm, but it could have been one hundred degrees or more inside the car and I wouldn't have noticed it. I had just "canned" one of those stories for which my station was famous.

Later that night, the catchy jingle set the opening visuals of Channel 5's 10:00 p.m. *Texas News* dancing across the television tubes of North Texas. The first story told of a school board meeting in Henderson County: "Brownsboro trustees shoot it out over longstanding disagreements." But the pictures of a Texas woman, her husband and her God wordlessly told what was really the whole story. Truly a story worthy of *The Texas News* from way down in East Texas.

The Crusading Reporter

On a blazin'-bright late afternoon in August, I was hard at work on the roof of the three-story building where I lived. A hot breeze had blown the fleecy, early morning clouds west toward the Permian Basin, scaring off everything that obscured the Texas sun.

In the hot, windy air, I was scrubbing my new Robert Hall suit and meditating that this clear, bright day was one of the darkest of my life.

My suit, a recent acquisition from Robert Hall's Men's Clothes, which boasted low prices because the clothes were displayed only on "plain pipe racks," dangled like a scarecrow on a makeshift clothesline. From a pail of sudsy water, I pulled a scouring brush similar to those used by the navy to swab the deck and brushed it ferociously on the suit pants and the tail of the suit coat. Duncan, WFC, watched with perverted amusement at his colleague's nausea at the revolting job.

Actually, the day had started quiet, even sleepy. Then, just a few hours ago, around midafternoon, before the downtown parking lots started emptying for suburban trips home, everything changed. In the city police pressroom on the third floor of the old cops and courts building, a beat call monitor was droning away with routing information about the 3:00 p.m. shift change. No breaking news there.

Johnny Rutledge, the night reporter for the *Dallas Morning News*, had just come on duty. As usual, he was quietly but thoroughly cleaning the phones and desks. With a bottle of antibacterial cleanser and the torn part of a worn-out bed sheet, he was sanitizing any item that a bacteria-laden dayside reporter might have touched. Johnny was one mean cleaning machine. He was possessed. He never even removed his signature big black cowboy hat before he attacked the germs at the start of his shift.

Other tenants in the room included two radio news announcers. A couple of television guys were dutifully checking the afternoon *Times Herald*. With no apologies, they would lift a story idea that a print reporter worked his ass off on and then rewrite it for television. Another reporter positioned himself where he could look out the window at the cars passing three stories below on Main Street. Every once in a while, he broke the silence with, "Ching a ling! Hot ding! Now that was a pair of legs!" Another reporter was trying to make time with a female caller who had innocently dialed a wrong number and got the pressroom, complete with a silver-tongued lecher. He spoke in a whisper to not wake the nap taker next to him. It was a slow afternoon. But everyone woke up when the monitor cracked with an alert for patrol cars: "102 and 103 with 604 [ambulance]. Got a major 7 at Main and North Central. Pedestrian struck." From the tone of the dispatcher's voice, it sounded like a really bad accident.

"Hell, that's just a couple of blocks down the street," Tom Matts blurted as he grabbed his tape recorder with the large KBOX letters on the side. He crashed the door space with two other guys, Keystone cops style.

I didn't get caught in the crush. I was trying to decide whether to take the news unit or make the dash on foot as the others did. The delay cost time. All the gear I needed was at hand, so I grabbed my camera and sprinted. In the hallway lined with doors separating the Criminal Investigation Division (CID) offices, a door to the burglary and theft bureau opened. Detective Butch Wilson, built like a warthog, stepped into my path. I slammed into him and bounced off without missing a step.

"Watch where your stupid ass is going," Butch spouted, adding for flavor and authentication, "We got your number and it's about up. You son-of-a-bitch!"

"Son of the Keystones is more like it," Rutledge suggested. He stayed behind to finish his cleaning. But I was on a tear. I wouldn't have stopped now for anything, much less to say I was sorry for the collision or respond to the insult to my mother.

But I did give a passing thought to the detective I just ran into and the "war" I seemed to be in and couldn't win. The whole police department, it seemed, was on a "Get Shipp" campaign—and had been for some time. I knew that all of this animosity was festering fallout following a series I wrote while I was with the *Times Herald* newspaper. The men behind the shields were not happy warriors. Well, I'd think more about the matter later, maybe with a cold Lone Star in hand. Right now, I had an accident to cover.

A shiver of fear streaked down my spine as I skipped the elevator ride, dancing two steps at a time down the stairs to Main Street. As I sprinted by the Western Union office, I could see lots of emergency lights a block to the east. Police units were cordoning off traffic on Central Expressway North. The ambulance was still there, but the closer I got to the accident the more I realized that the victim was already being loaded. Attendants slammed the doors shut. I had one chance: run fast and run the camera. At least I would have the ambulance pulling away. In my wildly jiggling viewfinder, I could see the "meat wagon" about to disappear around the corner. I was running down the middle of the street, my coattail flying straight out behind.

By god, I was getting the shot! But just as the ambulance turned the corner, I felt my feet leave the pavement. I hit something slick and was airborne. My contact with the concrete again was a crash landing when I hit the pavement and started a skid. Something slick was keeping me from righting myself. I had been so intent on keeping the departing ambulance in my camera viewfinder that I had neglected to notice my surroundings.

I couldn't stop to think of whether or how badly I was hurt. I wondered how much of the departing ambulance shot I'd salvaged. And was the camera damaged by the fall? When I stopped sliding, everything in my sight was out of focus, blurry. My foot slipped in my second attempt to right myself. I could still feel the mess under me.

With a heavy exaggeration of courtesy, a uniformed policeman said, "I would help you up, Mr. Shipp, but somebody might see me and think I cared. Oh, I care, but it's more for skunks and bad pennies. Sorry, Mr. Newsman. Besides, you are in pretty good shape for a guy who missed pictures of the body. All you have to do is take pictures of the stuff you are layin' in. More body here than they took to the hospital." Maniacal laughter echoed down Main Street's concrete canyon.

A garbage truck had hit and killed a man waiting to cross Central Expressway at Main Street. It seemed to be one of those freak accidents that happened because everybody's timing was off. According to a witness, ten seconds earlier the truck driver would have stopped at the red light instead of whipping left onto Central and hitting a hurrying pedestrian who'd left the curb too soon. He tripped as he tried to stop, realizing his tragic mistake. The news people were rapidly soaking up the colorful facts, as a witness recalled that the victim fell forward to be hit squarely by the multi-ton truck.

"The tires caused a cracking sound, like if it were eggs," the witness added, too specifically at least for a female radio reporter from KRLD. The witness's vivid recollections and the remains covering the back of my suit made that reporter seriously nauseous. She dashed behind a nearby bail bond building. Returning shortly, she grinned weakly and said, "August heat!"

One hour later, chastened and unhurt but angry, I was on my rooftop scrubbing my suit to get it clean enough to send to the cleaners.

"Duncan, get the hell outta' here," I lashed out at my overly interested cat. "You and your relatives never lose your nose for nastiness. Go round up one of your nice, clean rats." A fur ball factory making a nuisance of himself just added to a terrible day. At least most of the mess was gone. A good cleaner could take it from there.

I didn't feel like negotiating the fire escape and window back to my loft. I just settled down in the lengthening shade of the roof's outbuilding. Now Duncan appeared out of nowhere to get a quick, cheap head scratch and tummy rub. My skinny legs and flat stomach didn't make much of a lap, but Duncan didn't let that bother him as he stepped, turned and scooched around on what was there.

But getting back to the bad blood between me and the police…maybe I could think of a way to cool the ongoing war between me and certain members of the local constabulary. They really had burrs under their saddles, and I was the one getting the painful ride. I thought my righteous endeavors had taken a mysterious and mean turn immediately after what I had considered a clean hit on a wanton and scurrilous situation.

Several months earlier, I got the newspaper order to lead the charge that became a crusade to expose chinks in the police armor. The newspaper wanted a series of stories exposing the unethical, cavalier escapades of some otherwise pretty good cops. As a general assignments reporter, I got the dubious honor because editors always allowed regular beat reporters to have deniability when a bad story came up on their beat. Occupationally, they have to live there—on the beat. If they write the damning stories about the cops, then when the important stories emerge, the beat reporter finds himself with no source of information—or friends.

So when really scandalous stories pop up, headlines shout the wrongdoing over the byline of a lone, general reporter. In the city, police or fire departments, hides are nailed to the wall. Sometimes the mess is cleaned up. But the halls of the house of the guilty are filled with whispers and threats of "Who is this son-of-a-bitch who dug up this crap?" All the way from the police drinking trough at Club 66 on Jackson Street to the cop lockers in the basement of police headquarters at 2000 Main, the word is "remember the one who would screw with the Blue."

Incredibly, leading the charge damning the writer were the beat reporters who reentered the scorched territory acting as if they had nothing to do with it. They cursed the writer—me—the loudest. Of course, the cops never knew that it was the beat reporters who furnished many of the damning facts.

In the now cool shade of my third-floor rooftop, I recalled that news series that first displeased the police so much, igniting the war between me and the cops. In one installment, I exposed a citizens' crime watch group that had hatched into a love nest. A well-thought-of officer in charge of organizing the Northeast Dallas citizen crime fighters got drummed out of the ranks when word surfaced that the meetings had gotten out of hand and into bed. Apparently, the cops and their neighborhood volunteers, members of the citizens' crime watch group, were wife- and husband-swapping while they were supposed to be looking for and identifying burglars. It made a hell of a newspaper story.

The article that really brought the wrath of the brass down on my head, though, was a story about a mother-daughter hospitality house in Oak Cliff.

I wasn't, and still am not, certain, even to this day, what all was happening in the dwelling on Bonnet Boulevard. A nice-looking yellow house with gray trim, it looked like a bed-and-breakfast. Big American elm trees stood guard along the thoroughfare as one police car, and then another, came and went. After a short wait in the deep shade, the occupants with big guns and shiny badges were welcome visitors to the yellow house. The attractive middle-aged mother and her striking young daughter of voting age apparently loved uniforms.

As one officer put it, "There were a lot of suspicious calls made in Oak Cliff, logged to that address." My story pointed out the fact that there was always plenty of food available for the officers, on or off duty. "The daughter was right hospitable, very hospitable," one source said. "She was well schooled in giving the come-on look, and she flirted 'til her face cracked. She was really hot."

"She was especially careless with her dress. If you paid attention, it wasn't too long before you got to see what you thought you'd come for," he added.

But after the story was big news, department investigators concluded that the daughter was "all show and no go." Apparently, it was the mother who entertained backstage. My article was quick to point out that not all of the visiting law enforcement officers took advantage of the mother's charms.

After a while, I had it figured out. The ladies used food as bait, but the daughter was more bait than food. The officers hoped that some day, some time, she was going to give her mother a breather. But Mama was giving rides and riding high. And it was Mama who fell the farthest when happy hours ended at their hospitality inn.

I took a lot of pride in developing the mother-daughter story. There was lots of talk inside and outside the police department. My sources were hard to come by. Few people wanted to talk publicly about it. Editors were leery.

But it was the "Dead Men Tell No Tales" story that I least wanted to bring to print. As far as I knew, every reporter in town, especially police reporters, knew about the cemetery on Hatcher Street. Late at night, patrolmen would pull into the cemetery and tarry a while. Some caught up on their sleep. Others found various things to do, like read or study for the sergeant's exam. One officer repaired cars in that graveyard with a droplight plugged into a lighter socket. Of course there were lookouts and listeners who woke those who had a call on their beat. And others kept an eye out for suspicious supervisors. They alerted the cemetery gang when the bosses were in the vicinity. Incredibly, the supervisors knew all along what was up and did nothing about it. They probably had a deal of their own.

Doing a little investigating of my own, I found that the rumors were true. At two or three o'clock in the morning, traffic in and out of the cemetery was brisk—not heavy but steady. Actually, no one and nothing suffered if a call came in for a specific beat. It was always covered. The only dead people in this caper were already accounted for on nearby gravestones. After all, the guys figured, a little cemetery activity never hurt anyone.

Of course, when the city council and the city manager read the series, they did not agree. The "graveyard assembly" became a ghost group. The paper did an editorial condemning such disorderly conduct. Like all old news, the series was soon forgotten—almost. We news people liked to hang out with certain good-natured detectives, but even those cops refused to cut me an inch of slack. I was a pariah. I was told on more than one occasion that "it was fun to hate reporters and I was the most fun of all." Such animosity from people who had been friends made me angry enough to wish I'd mentioned other indiscretions, like the cute little red-haired cop who was spreading her charms among a select few officers who apparently found her worth the risk of serious trouble.

My good deeds uncovering scandal and corruption had backfired. This weighed on my mind. I figured I was just doing my job as my journalism training mandated. But sadly, I'd never be able to sit in the shade without reflecting on the repercussions of letting the sunshine in. It was the price that was charged to truth.

Now, in the relative comfort of my rooftop perch, my arm was tired from giving Duncan the deluxe rub, scratch and pat down. Then with a leap off my lap, Duncan executed the famous cat stretch. Forelegs out front with front feet firmly in place, his hind legs stretched way to the back. Now Duncan made a quick turnaround and backed up to the corner of the little building, making a quick spray on the wall. His territory was now strategically marked.

I watched him. Somehow, it is good therapy for a man to love an animal that appreciates it. It might just have been my imagination, but I thought Duncan planned it that way—a little animal comfort on one of the worst days of my life.

The State Fair Itch

E very once in a while, a photojournalist gets an idea that gnaws on his mind like a dog with a bone. No situation is too perilous, no odds too great to deter such an addict from seeking a fix or scratching an itch. Only crazed wolves and real photographers feel this sensation.

So it happened on one beautiful, fall day—the opening day of the Great State Fair of Texas—when I was called in for dayside duty. The fair opened the same way every year. It was boring television, to say the least. The hottest action was usually a bunch of nutty guys who, fittingly, called themselves Boneheads. Every year they closed the fair just as it officially opened. Same dumb thing, year after year. So when the editors assigned me to cover the "opening of the state fair" story, it seemed to me that they wanted somebody to put a new touch on an old tale.

I had never been happy with the usual "walking in the gate" shot from the sidewalk level, followed by the Big Tex footage and, finally, the swish-panning to the midway. I wanted an aerial shot, a panorama of the famous midway rides and carnival crowd. And I didn't want just an aerial shot of the midway—I had to have a midway shot from really high above it. I wouldn't have dared ask for the price of a plane. Editors would scream, "One shot?" A plane for one opening shot? A single establishing shot?" Now, with desire and a plan, I headed straight for the State Fair Electric Building. I had an idea, an itch that had to be scratched.

For me, a mental rash broke out every time I caught sight of the Electric Building tower at the fair. The tower is a kind of obelisk with a clock near its top. It casts a giant shadow as though a sun's finger is pointing out the grandeur of the huge grounds.

But it wasn't until I was inside the Electric Building tower—climbing up an aging wooden ladder with rickety one-by-four pine "rungs" somehow attached to the dark, cavernous structure's side—that I realized that my desire had been mixed with daring. Far up that dust-laden, sweltering tower, I could still look down and see Nancy Wylie, the public relations lady who went to so much trouble to get permission for me to embark on this foolish mission. I really didn't want to shout down to Nancy that I was within a heartbeat of backing out and returning to sanity and the safety of the ground.

I pondered these circumstances as I continued to climb another fifty feet. I was sweating like a mule in a bean barn and devoutly wished that I had curbed my enthusiasm to "change up" the state fair story. "Oh well, enough of that," I told myself as the nine-and-three-quarter-pound Bell & Howell that now swung from my wrist was beginning to feel like double its weight. The idiotic nature of this venture really came home to me when a loose rung—actually just a board—nearly came off in my hand. "How are you doing up there?" came a shout from the ground. The PR lady must have heard my expletive.

Her concern came just when I was seriously thinking about calling it quits. Darkness shrouded the ladder and surrounding walls. The atmosphere was starting to influence my thinking. It was suck-up time once more. I yelled to my ground crew of one that I was okay. I hammered the rung back tight with the butt of my camera, noting that it was a great camera. From then on, I had to count rungs to know when the loose one was next on the way down.

For the moment, I was glad I had left my Robert Hall suit coat hanging on a nail downstairs. Now, even my sweaty J.C. Penney shirt was starting to bind. Heat continued to build inside the tower. Some of that electric air conditioning on display down on the ground floor would have been wonderful. At that moment, what really felt good was sensing my approach to the top of the ladder. Sixty feet of terror was about to end as a platform-like structure became semivisible in a beam of renegade sunlight.

Only a few more steps were left. I would have rested, taken a breather, but the excitement of the coming view from the top demanded that I continue. I ascended the remaining steps. Dust was everywhere. Then I encountered another small obstacle. A lid fit over the opening onto the roof. Not a trapdoor or a cover—it was a lid with a top and sides. The only way I saw to exit the building was to put my shoulder up against it and push. I did. It gave way and flopped over in a puddle of rainwater on the roof.

Seconds later, I realized that way up here, half a football field off the ground, I had company. A bunch of yellow jackets had set up camp and were not interested in entertaining an uninvited guest. With the yellow jackets everywhere, I desperately wished now for the Robert Hall suit coat. I could use it for some serious swatting and then cover up like one of those suspects who doesn't want pictures taken. Slipping into a panic attack, I spotted the yellow jacket nest. I slipped off my Hush Puppy loafer and, with one swing, destroyed their home base.

With my shirt pulled up over my head, I now turned my attention to photography. I wound the camera, shot, shot and wound again, all the time making certain that the footage and exposure were correct. I even used all three lenses just for the hell of it, to get long, medium and tight shots. The worst torment on earth for a photographer is to go through a trying situation of filming and come up with a zero by making a stupid mistake.

I remembered a time in the news business, now legendary, when on these same fairgrounds a fellow newsman had his family and his camera here. Chuck Roast heard a yell and saw that firemen on a drill tower had run into trouble. Three men fell several stories to the ground. Instantly, Chuck positioned his camera and started rolling. It was raw drama. When it was over, he drove back to the TV station and ran into the newsroom. Totally out of breath, he excitedly opened his camera…to find it empty of film. He had never reloaded after a previous assignment. Thankfully, this did not happen to me on this opening day of the Great State Fair of Texas, when yellow jackets were stinging and ladder rungs were loose.

I never revisited the fairgrounds without recalling my self-generated aerial assignment. But I no longer had that yearning to scale my own Matterhorn. I can't remember if the editors were impressed with my panoramic shots.

But there were other stories of the state fair. During another season, I was in far South Oak Cliff one Saturday night. Some kid had driven his grandfather's Cadillac into Comb's Creek. I got the story and pictures. When returning to my news car and pulling out onto the road, I heard the ancient, one-channel police monitor going crazy calling for ambulances: "607, you and 608 go through the McKenzie Street gate. 601 and 602 come in off Parry." It went on until all of the ambulances were dispatched to…where? Those were fairground streets! It must be the fairgrounds! I had not been in television that long, but I knew news, having served on newspapers for ten years. But reporting and shooting on the run and all at the same time was scary, to say the least. And all of those ambulances being dispatched to the fairgrounds sent my heart racing.

On the police scanner, curiously, there were no ambulances checking out for runs to hospitals. That could be taken two ways: people were being treated at the scene, or all were dead. Now I was guessing: an amusement ride had gone bad, or some animal or machine had gotten loose and spooked a bunch of people.

My German news unit sped along from Kiest Boulevard to Corinth Street. Then I took the viaduct across to Forest Avenue. This brought me into the fairgrounds the back way by Pennsylvania Avenue. I whipped the Opel across the big parking lot back of the rollercoaster. In a second, I was up behind WRR's radio station. I had heard numerous ambulances check out there. Almost leaping from the car, I saw the grounds littered with people, all kinds, all sick.

The first person I spotted was the police PR guy, Art Hammer. "Art, what the hell is gong on here? Looks like that scene in *Gone with the Wind* with all the casualties on those tracks."

"Yep, but these people are just gut sick, or think they are. Apparently, the Town and Country Restaurant sold some bad éclairs—you know, those chocolate things with the cream filling," Art said, pausing. "There must be one hundred sick people scattered around here wanting medical attention. I doubt there were one hundred éclairs ordered in that place all day. Looks like we may have some opportunists in with the real ones. Probably figure they could get a few bucks just for throwing up. Hey, watch it! You are about step in some chocolate evidence."

I knew what Art was talking about. It usually happens around scenes like a city bus wreck. It starts out with eight people hurt on a bus when it has an accident. Before you know it, there are sixteen passenger/victims complaining of back pain. A good insurance check will make that pain disappear.

"The Texas State Fair is a great state fair"—so the song goes. And it is a great place for fun news. But watch out for yellow jackets and stay with the corny dogs. Leave the chocolate éclairs for the French.

Can't We All Just
Get Along?

The blonde in the skintight Levi's had a tired face, but she was good at her job, rushing burgers and shakes out to an asphalt lot full of cars at the Prince of Burgers. My eye focused more on the carhops than on the food as I gorged on a chili cheeseburger while waiting for the bus to rush my film story to Fort Worth. I am an average man, but my appetites for certain foods were gargantuan then, to say the least. Chili cheeseburgers topped the list, but I truly loved cornbread and lemon pie, tastes not usually satisfied at the Prince of Burgers. I did not believe in diets. Mostly I did not believe in hunger. When it came to food, I thought ahead. For example, I had already determined that this was a good time to get a bite to eat because it might be the only nutritious morsel I'd have time to eat for the rest of the day.

In my little Opel, I precariously balanced my burger basket, including its large order of French fries and my favorite strawberry malt, a drink so thick you could turn it upside down and it wouldn't spill. Mainly, I was trying not to dump the entire meal into my lap.

As I continued my juggling act, I noticed the carhop taking the orders of an Oldsmobile full of black folks in the next stall. She was as polite and courteous to them as she had been to me just a few minutes earlier. It was now 1959, and as a thoughtful and philosophical man, I couldn't help thinking just how far and fast the acceptance of an integrated society had gone in Dallas. A year or so ago in Dallas, blacks would not have been served car-side at the Prince of Burgers or at any other restaurant, fast or otherwise. They would not have been served at all unless they'd piled out of their cars and headed to the back of the restaurant. That's the way it was done. It had been that way forever.

I grew up in New Mexico, where the phrase "people of a different color" meant Indians and Hispanic people. I knew about black people from books. My mother read to me stories like *Little Black Sambo*. But as I remembered, Sambo's color was of little significance to me. Indelible in my mind were the scary situations that befell the little African hero. That such misfortunes could happen to a kid his age erased any awareness of the color of the child.

Not only was my understanding of different races limited, it also hardly occupied my country boy mind in those early years. Mostly, I thought about how soon a hole would wear in my "once-a-year" shoes or when the milk cows would come fresh and new calves would be 'round about. Slavery was a world away. Of much more immediate concern was where the nickel for the Friday afternoon movie was coming from.

I did remember my first encounter with a black person—a memorable occasion. Taking my first train ride with my six-year-old classmates, I traveled forty-eight miles in a passenger train from Artesia to Roswell, New Mexico. The reason for the trip has long since been lost, but I remember that it only cost each first-grade family a dime. I figured I would sacrifice seeing the Green Hornet's escape from death for one week.

In the Roswell depot, a popping, slapping sound caught my attention. Though the incident happened many years ago, it is as fresh in my memory as if it had happened last year. In an obscure corner, under a single, naked light bulb, was a shoeshine stand. At least I guessed it was a shoeshine stand, though I had never seen one before. But it had been mentioned in books.

I was fascinated. There really was a black man, like in the books. I can still recall how white his teeth were, and more intriguing were his white palms. The shine man never broke rhythm as he turned and gave me a warm smile. That smile would be imprinted on my mind for a long time.

When I was growing up, West Texas still had few black people. They mostly did domestic duties. Some had "good" jobs, like working in cotton gins. Others, like sharecroppers, labored on farms, plowing, cultivating and harvesting land that they would never own.

As I grew older, though, I realized that more and more often, derogatory terms were creeping into my neighbors' conversations in New Mexico, and later, Texas. Negroes were referred to as "Rastuss" when the name was Rayford. Or the white guy joked about the "coloreds and their watermelons" or "fighting with razors." Their children were often called "pickaninnies."

I was brought up by a mother who would not allow her children to say hurtful words about others, even when others did it. I carried her thoughts with me deep into the racist heart of Texas when I arrived in Dallas.

In the '50s, when I arrived to make my fortune in the city, Dallas was a "movin' up" place. The early powerbrokers, with names like Thornton, Wooten, Tatum, Florence and Rogers—all fantastic merchants, traders and businessmen—worked to make the city a mecca of prosperity in the Southwest. Their energy, planning and dealing moved Dallas from a smelly cattle crossing on the Trinity River to the sweet-smelling, very successful metropolis of big money and Neiman Marcus. They were giants—talented, hardworking and very lucky.

One of the favorite stories in city lore took root in their efforts in the '30s to get the nascent Texas Centennial Celebration located in Dallas. The Centennial Committee met in San Antonio. Houston and the Alamo City were among the competing cities. After the planning and dealing of the powerbrokers, Dallas made its bid. The Dallas group heard rumors that the city was very close to getting the nod. It was suggested that if they tossed in one more goodie, they would get the lucrative contract to be the site of the 1936 Texas Centennial.

R.L. Thornton, the banker, was sent in to play Dallas's trump card: an aquarium would be built on the site. The committee loved it. That was the clincher. Dallas got the Texas Centennial.

That night, the members of the winning contingent congratulated themselves in the easy chairs of the old, historic Menger Hotel. Sparkling flutes of champagne were lifted in honor of the victory and their own brilliance in pulling off the deal of the century. Finally, the conversation lagged as their euphoria waned. Banker Thornton had the last word. Born in a dugout carved from the banks of the Trinity

River and raised in the harsh poverty of the Texas prairie, he spoke through the curls of smoke and the intoxication of success: "Tell me, boys, what the hell is an aquarium?"

It was quiet in Dallas, at least, in 1959. This was not true in the rest of the nation. Up North, people were rioting. In the Deep South, blacks marched for their rights. Would it happen in Texas? The men who ran the city were confident that such things would not happen, saying, "Our Negroes are hardworking, God-fearing folks. They know when they're well off, and they're not prone to make trouble." This smug, self-satisfied opinion was accepted as reassurance, mostly by white people.

City fathers, called "the oligarchy" in certain quarters, sucked the smoke from their tightly rolled, four-bit cigars, sipped their bourbon and branch water from initialed glasses and spouted the "well-behaved blacks" theme. That was for the record. But in those same clubs high above the peaceful streets of Big D, there were other dealings.

I learned that these same wheeler-dealers intended to manage the integration of Big D. It would be done very quietly. No publicity. No fanfare. They all agreed that civic disturbances "would be bad for bidness." Summoning the black leaders of the community, they told them that, without whoopla or fuss, a change was about to take place. Black people would get on the city buses and sit down—anywhere. No more going to the back of the bus. Tranquility was the word. The colored lady who usually lugged her big, heavy shopping bag up several flights of stairs to the far balcony in the movie house would walk in and set her bag right down beside her on the main floor of the best theater in town. The "colored only" and "white only" signs would be removed from drinking fountains in commercial and municipal buildings. In return, the leaders of the black community promised that there would be no demonstrations or other disturbances. And there would be no publicity.

Down tumbled the barriers that had separated white from black for so long. Nothing was printed in the newspapers. Not a camera shot on television news or a story on radio. That was the way the deal had been struck. The Dealeys and the Chambers, owners of the newspapers, stuck by their guns. Not a breath of the "I" word in Dallas. Peace prevailed.

But a renegade cowboy in Fort Worth, who was a major mover there, hated Dallas. Much bad blood flowed between Amon Carter, the rich newspaper publisher and owner of much of Fort Worth, and the sister city to the east. The *Fort Worth Star Telegram* carried constant stories about the way desegregation was working in Dallas as well as Fort Worth. Blacks were registering for rooms in downtown hotels. Restaurants were accommodating black diners. The Fort Worth press was much noisier than the Dallas press.

Actually, I worked for Amon Carter as a reporter in the Dallas bureau of WBAP-TV Channel 5, the first and finest local television news department in the nation. It was owned and operated in Fort Worth by the Amon Carter family. WBAP was thorough in covering the news. And integration in Dallas was certainly news.

Of course, the inevitable happened when stories of the Dallas activity, or lack thereof, became national items. Even the smoothest transitions will generate opposition. Several groups and individuals created opportunities to enhance their positions by posturing and doing a little speechmaking in Dallas, saying that the town "wasn't moving fast enough" in their direction. They probably thought that a little exposure in this fertile field just might increase the coffers of several black organizations.

In no time, then, Channel 5 newsmen were following demonstrations in Dallas of students from the college campuses in East Texas and a few from South Texas, around Houston. These incidents never blossomed into the stuff that made newsmen's reputations. Neither did the sit-ins at the Greyhound bus station.

One afternoon, though, things did become nasty when the manager of the bus station, a giant of a man, decided that he didn't want me shooting pictures of a handful of black people seated at the depot's lunch counter.

"I'm going to physically put your ass on the next bus out if you don't take your trashy little camera and your silly business out of here right now!" warned this mountain of a guy, appearing to me to be as big as one of his buses. I probably should have tucked my 16mm under my arm and vacated the troubled area. But I was feeling a little mulish that afternoon. I got a new, fresh wind on my Bell & Howell and just continued taking pictures.

The station master meant it. He grabbed me by the belt and ushered me out to the departure area, tossing me headfirst into the open luggage area of an eastbound bus. Luckily, the other side of the bay was also open. I was up and out of there before the last announcement of departures for Terrell, Tyler and other points east.

The bus station episode was the beginning. It proved to be the catalyst for my association with the black freedom movement in the Southwest. The next incident involved an itinerant preacher and two black fellow travelers. They targeted a food place "holdout" called H.L. Green's, a downtown, low-priced, variety department store. Its lunch counter, in an obscure area of the store, had always served anyone seated there. But blacks usually got poor or slow service and insulting attitudes. I decided to do an "integration story" about the preacher and his friends at the H.L. Green lunch counter.

The short, muscular man with bushy eyebrows and a turned-down mouth in charge of the lunch counter told me in no uncertain terms not to invade the privacy of the dining area while the preacher and his friends nursed a couple of cheap, cold cups of coffee. "You will end up out in the street if you don't listen to what I tell ya, hear?"

I was not "mulish" this hot August afternoon. I was what the boys down at the poolroom call "pissed full of it." I had been hammered, pushed and pulled. I'd had degrading things shouted at me because, like a lot of other people, I saw the reality of segregation. With my pictures, I could hold a mirror up for the city to see. And I thought that just maybe one of these white Neanderthals might just cut me a little slack.

I just stared at the doltish figure, whose nose curved downward from his dull eyes. By then I'd had enough. I slipped a nickel into a nearby pay phone and called WBAP's Dallas bureau in the county pressroom. My partner, Dan Owens, silent Dan, answered. I laid out my plan for recording a lunch counter interview, despite the manager's admonitions. Dan said I could count on him if trouble started. Trouble started.

The manager sprang into action when I went back to the lunch counter area and started filming. I felt a powerful hand grab me by the nape of the neck. Another hand firmly grasped the seat of my Robert Hall suit. I felt a fleeting panic that the cloth could not withstand such a test. Like a two-man comedy team, we tripped and skipped down the aisle toward the front door. I glanced toward a nearby rack of merchandise. There was silent Dan, camera rolling at sixty-four fast frames per second, the two-inch lens barely peeking out through a dainty selection of ladies panties. He was getting all the action.

The store's self-appointed bailiff shouted, "Somebody open that front door!" Somebody did, and that burly lunchroom manager tossed me onto the sidewalk like a pitchfork of hay. With the force of the toss, the momentum rolled me across a wide sidewalk to the curb. Then the sound of screeching brakes pierced the quiet afternoon along Main Street. The driver of a city bus thought that I was about to roll into the street in front of the White Rock Limited. It was close.

A little shaken, I waved a salute of thanks toward the quick-thinking, relieved bus driver. I dusted myself off. No real hurt places, and my Robert Hall suit was no worse for the toss. The whole time, Dan was rolling his film. For the 6:00 p.m. news, WBAP-TV had one of the most vivid stories to come out of the integration struggle.

Maybe it's a tribute to my upbringing in New Mexico, but I never held a grudge against the people who made my job so hard. Actually, I developed a cordial, if not close, friendship with the moose at the bus station. After all, I figured, they have a right to do what they have to do—and so do I.

"Integration" also became a familiar word around the Dallas Independent School District as desegregation took place under a court order. The agreed-upon rule was "force but no violence."

But in the city, there were other incidents. One turned out to be ridiculous. One afternoon, local Black Panthers members, ashamed that their northern chapters were doing nothing, took over a large South Dallas supermarket, home of a large portion of Dallas's black residents. They announced to the black customers, "We're going to trash old whitey's place!" "Old whitey's place" was the only real grocery store in the vicinity. The neighborhood residents appreciated and treasured the place. They rebelled at the command and quickly turned on the Panthers, pinning them to the floor and holding them until the law arrived.

Through the next few years, there were, inevitably, some marches and demonstrations in Dallas. Several organizations cried in a repetitive chorus that the African Americans were not getting all that they should. But change was on the march, and it came to Dallas. It was not always smooth, but the city avoided the violence and bloodshed that characterized too many other cities. As for me, I continued to observe the black race's march to equality and concluded that over those years there appeared to be a whole lot more black businessmen than shoeshine men.

The Darling of the Police Department

T he only thing stirring in the police pressroom on a midweek
morning was a noisy fly. This outhouse insect with the charmed life,
or one of his pals, had been buzzing the stale atmosphere of the "cop
shop" for what seemed like several months. The oversized green fly, the
kind often found tormenting country folks, must have found the climate
at least somewhat agreeable. The only danger it faced was from *Times
Herald* police beat writer George Carter. George had just about worn out
a handful of tattered, rolled-up police complaint sheets trying to kill that
pesky buzzer.

But this police reporter was out of pocket when an oak-sized detective
lumbered into the pressroom looking for him. When he was informed
by an early morning radio newsman who kept up with such things that
George was probably at Mike's barbecue and beer stand across Harwood
Street, the detective slapped his big meat hook of a hand against a desk. It
awakened the other radio man and startled Julia Scott, a black newspaper
reporter. *Dallas Morning News*'s veteran Jim Ewell had just shown up for
work. He didn't flinch at the detective's antics. You couldn't spook Jim
with a starter's pistol. He was one cool customer, with his pipe stuck in his
face. Without directing his comment to anyone in particular, he looked at
his watch and said, "George is on his second pack of smokes and is asking
Mike to pull the lid on his sixth beer of the day."

"I need one of you Ms. Americas to witness a statement down in burglary," the burly policeman announced. He popped those giant hands together, clapping again to make certain he maintained our attention. "Bert, how's about you gracing us with your company and writing skills," he said. "Hear you are the new department darling as of the other night down on St. Louis Street."

As usual, I was available. Of course, like all television reporters, I did it all—police, city hall, schools and anything else. Newsmen set up shop around the police station because that's usually where the action was at that time of day. In general, the news business was spread between killings, burglaries, wrecks and 7-Eleven robberies. Some television journalists made a living off car accidents. If a fellow could get to a wreck before his competitors, he was held in high esteem.

"Glad to be of service, Mr. Detective," I said. "Helping out detectives is becoming my thing." No smart comments about "department darling." I hoped my comment threw off anything the detective might have insinuated. The less said, the better. Concerning the "department darling" thing, I would just as soon have the loudmouth detective zip his lip. St. Louis Street was a scary situation a few nights ago, one that I preferred to forget.

That night, I was alone in the county pressroom. Most of the time, night duty in WBAP's Dallas bureau was uneventful. This was one of those nights. It had started painfully dull and appeared to be moving toward comatose. It was still fairly light but drawing dark fast when lights flickered on a special police radio channel. I heard cops talking about some urgent ugly business taking place around St Louis Street, slightly south of the downtown area. I had heard enough police talk. I figured a bunch of vice squad guys were about to interrupt business at a whorehouse.

"A whorehouse raid!" I shouted as I snatched up my camera. "Lordy, I'd better grab the light," I reminded myself. The dayside reporter had left it on "charge" after draining out all the juice on another assignment. No telling how much charge it still had in it. I had to take a chance. It was the only light on the premises.

I zipped through downtown on Main Street. Homebound traffic had pretty much drained off. A few talented office chicks might be late leaving, taking advantage of the two-for-one cocktails at the Turf Bar happy hour. I whipped south on Harwood and found the light at Commerce in my favor. The Jackson Street signal was somewhere between amber and red. I voted for amber and headed for Wood Street. That light was totally, unequivocally red. Then I sped toward the Farmers' Market area. What a house of ill repute was doing on the edge of the Farmers' Market trade zone was something I never could figure out.

I pulled my little orange news wagon up an alley behind some trash c ans. My position was close to the action but not close enough to be noticed. I was aware of a number of "smooth" cars, police cars without markings, "unwrapped" as they were called. The sun had pretty much gone down, but there was more than enough cop car light to flood the area.

After a minute or two, I thought the raid had already taken place. The cops were yelling at women who were being shoved into a panel truck. Some men, who might have been customers, were getting the "what for" for patronizing and consorting with "such uglies." I remained in the deep shadows, careful not to become part of the story if one was to develop.

Then I saw a husky, bald, black man acting like a jackass. Every time a cop would get a hand on him, he jerked loose and took a swat at the officer. The cops were too busy to notice me, even though I was filming all of the action. I could that tell the light battery should have been charged a lot longer. It was fading fast, really getting weaker. I was thirty yards away, now in deep dark. I had no idea if I was picking up anything at all, but if I was getting any pictures, they might be pretty good. The black male subject was being screamed at and told to "behave." He was huge and, even above the police noise, sounded pretty mean. It turned out that he was the man of the whorehouse, the pimp. He was roughly subdued and firmly cuffed, with his hands behind him. I saw all of this, but I didn't know if or what I was filming.

Then the prisoner made a lunge at one of the detectives. He flattened the cop, who landed with a cloud of dust. "You son-of-a-bitch!" Then, with a flash of orange fire, a gunshot from the cloud of dust split the night.

I froze. I was really scared. Was my camera running? Was my light still good? I had no idea. In an instant, things went from bad to worse.

"You dumb shit, he's handcuffed!" an officer shouted in the dark at the shooter.

The prisoner dropped like he was shot, badly shot. Someone hollered for an ambulance. Now someone noticed that there was a dim television camera light. Cops know that where there is a TV camera light, there is a newsman to go with it. "Oh, shit! Who's over there with the light? Cut it off! Now! We mean NOW!" the voice demanded.

I was within a few feet of the writhing, mortally wounded pimp. The detective with the gun was quickly deprived of it. Now the cops focused their attention on me. "What's your name and what are you doing here?" a patrol lieutenant demanded.

I thought, ridiculously, "You are not in a good position to be rude." I knew now what I had really seen. A cop had just shot a handcuffed prisoner in cold blood. Earlier, I had just thought that might be what I'd witnessed. Now I knew.

"Hey, I know him. It's what's-his-name from over at Channel 5. Used to be bad news at the *Times Herald*." Detective Roscoe Borger took over. "Did ya get all that on film?" he asked cautiously.

"Can't tell," I covered myself. "I might have been too far away. The old light may not be what it used to be. Needs a charge every once in a while to get it up, like a lot of us." I tried to inject a little levity into the tense atmosphere.

I knew I might be in trouble no matter what I said. I wondered if I might be "rubbed out" just to keep me quiet. I'd learned a lot about police doings when I was a reporter in Abilene. But then Abilene was a place where anything was likely and not always fair.

I kept my mouth shut and let the cops think what they would. Then I got the hell out of the neighborhood and off to Fort Worth as fast as my four cylinders could get to the end of the turnpike.

The ten o'clock news on Channel 5 was the only station to have the shooting. The story started with pictures of the body being loaded into the ambulance. The story reported, "Police are still trying to untangle the events surrounding the shooting of the operator of a house of prostitution tonight on Dallas's south side." No harm to the department in that report. The ball was now on the police side of the net. But what about the shooting pictures? Did they not turn out? Was it too dark? I never found out, but the pictures I thought I shot never showed up on the news.

Speculation among police people was that Shipp "lost" them. The police department, of course, had to come up with its own final chapter to the story. So, weeks later, after an in-house investigation and grand jury attention, the police decided that the shooting was in self-defense. I kept my silence. Shortly after that, I noticed that I now had the run of the police department. No door was closed. Files were opened. News tips came from everywhere. I was the golden boy of the police.

When I followed the detective back into the burglary bureau interrogation room, the bureau captain gave me the old thumbs up sign. And before I had completed my witnessing business, I was "howdy'd" by a half-dozen normally sober, sour-faced detectives. The word was out that I had "dumped" the shooting pictures and saved a cop's ass. But as I signed my name to the suspect's confession, I thought to myself, "I wonder what I would have done if I had had the pictures on the film." I'd never know. Neither would the officers who called me a "darling."

I noticed that the prisoner who had just given a statement looked like he might have been the loser in a one-legged, free-for-all ass-kicking contest. He was badly bruised, to say the least. I started reading the statement.

The suspect's name was Finis Blanketview. He said he was an Irving plumber. He developed an interesting side action when he decided to case property as a plumber and then plunder it as a burglar. Unfortunately, the territory that he plundered belonged to the French boys, a notorious gang from the Balch Springs area south of Dallas. Having for some time staked out the Denton Road industrial district, they were the best burglars in the business. And these boys had no need for a partner.

When they got wind of Mr. Blanketview's plans to help himself to some of their action, they laid in wait, hijacked the intruder and then just beat the holy crap out of him. They left him tied up inside a heavy machinery warehouse and called the cops.

I put the police "beef" sheet back in order and replaced the paper clip. I looked at Finis, wanting to laugh. How could a guy be so dumb? Then I had a great idea. It wouldn't hurt to ask. "How would you like to be the main man in a television news story about burglary?" Finis was happy to oblige. In the subsequent TV documentary, Finis was the star, acting more like a hero than a petty thief. And my standing with the police was only enhanced.

The inevitable result of this fame happened about a year after I first met Finis. A deputy sheriff from Bill Decker's office called me. "Ya hear about the robber who held up a bank down in Mansfield and is now holed up in an old flophouse hotel in downtown Cleburne?" The deputy continued, "Well, get this. He's keeping a bunch of lawmen at bay and says he'll give up if you will come down there and walk him out."

I was totally astonished. The Johnson County sheriff radioed the Dallas Sheriff's Department and told them to get "that television newsman" down there. I wasted no time getting to downtown Cleburne. Of course, the little orange unit was flanked front and rear with police vehicles with sets of lights and sirens.

As I wriggled my way through the crowd, I had "interview" on my mind. Lugging my big camera and managing the sound camera, too, I shouted from the edge of the crowd. "Finis, that you up there? I'm comin' up. Okay, Finis?" It took several attempts to get a response. But there it came rather weakly: "Come on up...by yourself."

I read every face as I made my way through the crowd. I wanted no unexpected moves. I knew county sheriffs and their deputies. They *made* the law and they *were* the law. And they would keep order. Fortunately, I didn't notice anyone who was about to try foolishly to become a hero. Probably they figured there was going to be only one hero this day. Just who was yet to be determined, even if it cost one television newsman.

Thank goodness Finis was in a room on the second floor. That sound gear was a hernia-maker. "Finis, I'm here. Open the door before I drop this stuff!"

"By yourself?" Finis asked, as he eased the ancient, creaking door open enough for me to squeeze in. "Oh! Excuse me! I didn't open it enough. Got your interview camera, I see." He spoke knowingly, remembering the interview from his glory days on television.

One of the best lines in the interview was Finis saying he'd "rather surrender to the French gang than give up to that pack of police wolves down there." Poor Finis. He really wasn't a bad guy. Just not too smart—or lucky. I got my exclusive interview and a little glory. Finis got safe passage to jail without getting shot. As I passed through the curious and relieved crowd, I thought it really did pay to be a plumber's friend!

When the story ran, the French boys laid low. Finis practically ruined their business. Now they had to sleep with one eye open. Mr. Blanketview and I did not become good friends, but we were now firm acquaintances and colleagues in the television business.

As I sped up Main Street, I remembered that the last time I was here, it was also on a law and order mission. It was during my newspaper days, and the school was being integrated, not too peacefully. One Texas Ranger was brought in to keep the peace. Just like Lone Wolf Gonzalez of yesteryear, he was "one Ranger for one riot." A newsman could do worse than have ties to the police.

TV News as a Contact Sport

R oy, ya better take the lid off another Pearl," I whined to the Press Club bartender. My ribs hurt like someone had punched me good. But sitting on a comfortable lounge stool drinking free, cold beer was excellent therapy for a sore anything. For sure, it was good medicine for injured ribs.

It was a lousy, gray Friday afternoon. Downtown was winding down as the week came to an end. News was also winding down. I was just another reporter working nights for the *Dallas Times Herald*. All of the day's stories, shipped on the Turnpike Express from Dallas, were now on Fort Worth's editing benches. Shipping the film and the written stories on the bus sure beat having to drive thirty-five miles.

Roy popped the lid off my third beer. The sound of the lid leaving a longneck is almost as delightful as the taste of the brew itself. And the fact that it was going on Dan Edward's tab made the imbibing even more pleasurable. I knew Dan wanted it that way or he wouldn't have said, "Continue to nurse yourself back to health. I've got to go out and win The Salvation Army some new friends."

Dan handled public relations for The Salvation Army. He made lots of friends for the Army with his expense account. Dan also made them lots of money. So when the booze bills came in, the Army brass paid them. I drank one to the Army, too. Salute!

As I sucked down the second big swig of the disappearing Pearl, the Press Club entrance door blasted open. One of the tallest, smartest women ever to grace the Press Club made her entrance. Pat Zhardt was welcome in any newsroom and public relations outlet in Dallas.

Swaggering up to the bar, she shed her coat and smoothed out a couple of skirt wrinkles. Ms. Zhardt, of Braniff Airways fame, said baldly to me, "Heard ya got the crap whipped out of you down at the sheriff's place today. It's all over the radio. Guess you will be big on the six o'clock news. Boy, you are always right in the middle of it when the fighting starts. Gimme a scotch, Roy."

Pat was right. I sighed and winced at the pain in my battered ribs. I always seemed to be at the right place at the wrong time or the wrong place at the right time. A newsman getting whipped up always seemed to be newsworthy, especially when accompanied by fine action pictures.

To be sure, I didn't mind a little publicity. I was just another reporter, writing for the *Dallas Times Herald*. I had never made the roster of noted newsmen, either now or earlier, as editor of a small suburban newspaper. But when I switched from print to television, I opened the curtain on a new stage, peopled with new characters, more colorful and eager for their moment in the electronic sun. But I was not eager to be part of the story, only the recorder of the tale.

"You got pounded the other day down at the cop shop, didn't you?" the airline lady remembered. "I was sipping with a police reporter, and he said maybe you egged the suspect on a little. Matter of fact, the reporter told me that old Ira Trantham, the cop, let his prisoner loose on ya after he heard you kinda aggravating the guy. You weren't up to anything like that, were you?" Pat teased.

"Me? Who, me? Pat, you know I'm pure as a rose. I'm full of peace. Just a television news reporter trying to make an honest living," I bantered with her. "Besides, I need all the ribs I can protect. Does seem to happen a lot. Remember that Oklahoma lawyer who popped me real good down at the federal courthouse a month or so ago? He was losing and messing up the Billie Sol Estes case so bad that he had to take his frustrations out on somebody. I just happened to be in his way. By the way, I made the New York papers with that little bout."

Pat readjusted those long, freckled legs with another crossover while patting her cloud of red hair to match the balance of her body. She was one big ole gal. Not the kind you would lust over, but always a good buddy, a friend. She was smart and a real hard worker.

From what I heard, Pat had to be a hard worker. Word was that her husband ran off and left her with a baby. She got on at Braniff 'cause an idiot or two out there didn't care to work that hard. When Braniff's Electra planes crashed in the scrub woods of Central Texas and the cornfields of Indiana, Pat was pushed through the doors of news conferences to explain what happened. The big bosses would hide behind the curtains while Pat took the punches and won the respect of media people.

"Want some more medicine for those ribs? I think Dr. Braniff could afford to prescribe a dose," Pat offered. I accepted with my usual appreciation. "What hurt ribs?" I winced when I laughed, holding a Pearl up in a toast. "There's real healing power in those Salvation Army beers."

"Speaking of getting in trouble with your news objects," Pat continued, "I swear I still laugh when I think about the column that Fairfax Nesbit wrote about you in the *Morning News*. She had a running total of the times you got jumped on. Is it nine or ten times? I think it's funny, though, knowing what a peaceful and charming person you really are."

"Pat, have another scotch, and Roy, put it on the Army's tab," I interrupted. "I do like the charming bit. But peaceful, I don't know. I'm sorry. Go on about Fax's column, please."

"What I was saying was that, of all the times you have been pounced upon, the funniest was that time outside Judge Joe B. Brown's courtroom. Remember when the kid on trial was really getting worked over by the prosecution? Then his grandmother was ushered from the courtroom because she was using her bad mouth to work over the DA's assistant?"

"Yeah. Oh yeah!" I recalled that incident. "That wiry, little old piece of fence post. I'll bet she was eighty and built roads until she was seventy-five. Tough! Oh, my Lord, she was tough! I didn't pay her much mind until I felt this huge lump on my back. I was out in the hallway, minding my own business, taking pictures through a window. Then came this war whoop. Sounded like a battle cry, complete with, 'You low-grade, unwrapped sons-a-bitches!' What that meant I have no idea, nor did I care, 'cause that old lady landed on my back like a jockey. At the same time, she started slapping my sides with her worn-out purse. I think all I saw was those old tortoise-shell handles when she flipped it from side to side."

"Yep, that was the way Faxie pictured it in her column," Pat snickered. "I just howled. I could see you running up and down that hall trying to get that monkey woman off your back. She was riding you like a pony."

She turned to the bartender. "Roy, I could use a dram of the 'old isle' to get me home. So I don't get so aggravated at the traffic. If I have a little taste of tolerance I won't become a hostile road warrior." She waved a final goodbye. "See ya, tough guy. And remember what my old grandpappy used to say: 'Stay down for the full count. Ya might could use the rest.'"

"Bye, Pat. Keep them Electras in the air. Those cornfields aren't any place to be landin' a load of payin' customers," I countered, but in a fading voice that only Roy could distinguish. Pat was not the type to josh over planes falling out of the sky.

While the town was winding down on this Friday afternoon and evening, the possibility of an item for the ten o'clock news was getting more remote. I remembered that there might still be some goings-on down at the federal building, where a long-suffering subcommittee was hearing testimony regarding the trafficking of women of ill repute. White slavery, some called it.

I decided to run down to the hearings and at least look over the crop of witnesses who had been rounded up for the sessions. Pimps, whores and sons-a-bitches from Lord knows where were on the docket. No locals, I noticed. The ladies looked pretty good, though they had that tough demeanor that goes with their business.

There was a surprising air of jubilation, even merriment, in the granite and marble hallway. Then, as I approached the corner of another hall, it occurred to me that it wasn't cheap perfume I detected. It was wine, the sweet-smelling product of the grape. "No wonder 'we' are feeling sorta' lively so late on Friday afternoon," I mused, rolling a little "ah ha" through my mind. How about a few feet of film for a story on how federal witnesses spend their time while waiting to testify? It could be one of those stories *Texas News* editors love to fiddle with—an off-the-wall saga.

With the camera rolling, I cruised the first hall, where a party atmosphere was in full swing. The ladies were having a fine time. At first the girls paid me little mind. There were even a few come-hither looks for the Bell & Howell. One painted doll even blew the lens a kiss.

Then came the queen of the ball. She was a big blond, a really big, green-eyed blonde, later identified as Trudy Green. What a piece of work she was! Six feet tall, with stiletto spike heels, painted up like a clown in a three-ring circus. Actually, she didn't really appear to need all that paint. She was good-lookin'.

Suddenly, out of nowhere, without provocation or invitation, her frivolous side seemed to go crazy. She turned the west hallway into a war path. With high heels clacking and a big wad of gum popping, she came down the hall swinging a large white purse with straps like David might have had on his slingshot.

Trudy appeared to be loaded. She could have been on "Sweet Lucy" most of the day and popped a pill or two to drown the boredom. She was out to show her fellow travelers how to liven up the place. Those high heels *clip-clopped* against the hard tile floor. She had a full head of steam, eyes focused on the camera. She was about to make the 10:00 p.m. news!

"Boy! What a shot this is gonna make!" I thought as I looked through the viewfinder to see that big plank of a woman lumbering toward me. She swung that purse, winging it straight toward me. "What a picture!" As she got right on top of my shot, she swung the purse for the finale. Crash! Right against my head! It was like a rock. I heard something break and saw falling stars and flying swirls. Trudy had just about turned my lights out. I staggered to a bench as that blonde gave me a swift kick to the shin and another whack with her handbag, now dripping with a liquid that looked and smelled like the product of California vines. Couldn't be much "Sweet Lucy" left. The blonde bull must have ingested most of it. In her radiator, it was a powerful, mean fluid. Swat! Kick! Kick! Swat! She focused her rage on me, a person who was running out of film and good sense.

Taking all of this in were U.S. Marshals Leonard Everett and Henry White and federal bail bondsman Will Soltis. As things stood, they weren't on the fight card. It was, for the moment, a spectator sport enjoyed by the male spectators and even two of the women. Trudy was at the top of her form. She really intended to take this television news animal down. Then it became a free-for-all as the other ladies joined in. With at least three of the women beating up on me, the melee now caused some concern for the marshals and Will Soltis. They heeded the call to arms.

Everett grabbed Big Trudy. Big Trudy grabbed Marshal Everett. She was fairly young. He was getting up there—maybe sixty-five. Now they had a new fight. Two other girls, Tina Martinez and Lisa York, jumped Soltis and White. Spectators swarmed in from everywhere and reaped a rousing reward. What a fight! I recovered in time to reload and roll the camera again. Got good stuff, too, along with a few bruises.

Finally, the courthouse hall was brought back to order. The girls were cuffed and celled, protesting to everybody within hearing distance that they were none too pleased with this turn of events. Besides, they were out of wine. On their way to the cellblock, they were still cursing "the newsman who started all this."

I never heard them. I was on my way to Fort Worth. It was too late for the bus, but this time, the trip was worth it. I made the 10:00 p.m. news, and the pictures were nothing short of sensational. The "ladies" were charged with assaulting federal officers, and lawmen could not have been more pleased.

Trudy told Marshal White that she was going to get her boyfriend to "kill that long-nosed, skinny, son-of-a-bitch of a newsman." The marshal later told me that if that was her biggest worry now, she had a surprise coming. How about five years in the slammer?

"I wouldn't worry one hour about Trudy Green or her boyfriend," he said. "Matter of fact, with Trudy in federal prison, she probably doesn't have a boyfriend anymore. She was his bread and butter on the street. And if he kills you, we'll put him away, too." Somehow I was not reassured.

The worst thing to come out of all of this was that when Judge Atwell and Judge T. Whitfield Davidson got wind of the ruckus, they eliminated any filming in the federal courthouse. That was a real loss. The incident later became known as the "out in the cold" caper. After that, camera people froze their butts off standing outside on the St. Paul Street side of the courthouse.

It was late, but I made it back to the Press Club in time to have Roy pull the top off another cold one. I raised my arm in salute to the screen as my story led the ten o'clock news. My arm was still sore. So were my ribs.

Tim's Shoes

A tourist gone far astray could make a wrong turn and end up there. News reporters find too many stories involving violence there. Poverty fighters find fertile fields for their work there. No matter how a person ends up there, the western section of Dallas is an experience not requested and never, if possible, repeated.

A deep depression seeped into my soul as I urged my cold-natured news unit across the unsightly Trinity River. The big, dirty ditch is part of what separates Dallas's "haves" from "have-nots." A misnamed Continental Boulevard merges into an unkempt Singleton Boulevard on the west side of the aging bridge. I had always thought that the grandiose name of "boulevard" should be applied to more affluent streets, not ugly thoroughfares running through pockets of poverty that empty into slums.

The structures lining Singleton Boulevard reflected the lives of the inhabitants: old and beaten down but still, incredibly, with a thin thread of hope. Decrepit service stations were run by down-and-outers who apparently still believed in working for a dollar. Unsightly junkyards were watched over by men in worn overalls who figured that one day they, too, might get a break. The scene was dotted with paper-thin houses. Mothers and fathers worked from daylight to dusk so that someday their offspring could escape this prison of poverty.

In a way, I could relate to these people. I came from circumstances similar to theirs. Maybe they weren't this austere, but I knew what it was like to have one pair of shoes that had to last all year. At school, I ate onion sandwiches out of a paper sack while many of my classmates munched on store-bought white bread with high-priced potted meat. I could see the salad dressing oozing from around the crust of the soft white bread. Their lunches were neatly packed with a banana or apple in a tin lunchbox featuring Orphan Annie's or Captain Midnight's picture on the outside.

But I figured that my formative years and the circumstances that accompanied them were really "no big deal." My mother and grandmother kept me in clean underclothes and overalls. There were always home-style haircuts. Wounds of disappointment were always doctored with the salve of promise. When things were bad, there was always the goodness of "better tomorrows." And when things really hurt, there were kisses to make them well. I always believed that I could "live on homemade love." In my dark hours, my mother looked at me with her beautiful blue eyes and whispered, "Everything's going to be all right." And it was, too.

Sometimes it seemed that the whole of West Dallas believed that the hole of despair could be filled with promises, better tomorrows and love—love like that of Brother Bill Harrod. He was a country-style preacher who didn't stoop to reach those who came to see what kind of deal he had with God. To the people of West Dallas he preached the promise of better times to come.

To the youngsters he always gave shoes. Once a year, after ding-donging the merchants of big-hearted Dallas for money and merchandise, he threw a wingding of a shoe party. Every year, the affair was scheduled to correspond with the Christmas season. It was nearly always accompanied by a severe cold spell, but there were never any complaints as the youngsters lined up for a warm pair of unscuffed shoes—with shoestrings.

Whether it was the luck of the Scotch-Irish or just a bad draw, as a reporter I felt that I always drew the assignment when it was a "poor people" story. I didn't mind the topic, but it always seemed that the weather was as derelict as the subjects. Actually, I liked the "people" stories. They were real. You could get your meat hooks into facts and circumstances. But it did seem like more of my stories took place in the wind, the cold and other hostile atmospheres than in any other climate.

Today was bitterly cold. But inside Brother Bill's little old church, where shoe dreams came true, it was as warm as the old minister's heart. The line for the footwear trailed out the front door to the cold outside. The eager children stood like a frozen fence that picketed out of the church building, down crumbling concrete steps and out into the bare yard.

The ground was rock-hard with a glistening crust of ice as the thermometer hovered a degree below freezing. A biting north wind gnawed at exposed fingers and noses. I was experiencing all of this as I wrote the story in my mind. I was mentally matching the scene with my film shots. The wait was tortuous, but the prize of a pair of new, shiny shoes made the torment worth the wait. At least that's what the little "kidcicles" told my rolling camera through chattering teeth. Stomping feet gave me another action shot, while clapping hands added a nice touch. Missing gloves told another story.

In the frigid air, my camera panned along the waiting line. It was extremely long. When I came to the end of the human chain, I almost didn't see a very small boy, his hands crammed down in a pair of well-worn jeans. He wore a thin, cloth coat, no hat and shoes that barely covered his feet. I had my story.

If there was one kid in that pathetic chain who had a real reason to be there, it was that boy. He said that his name was Tim, soon to be seven years old. His pleasure was infectious. "I'm going to get me some new shoes!" he said. His need for shoes was as severe as the weather. The shoes he had on his feet were next to nothing. They had once been brown, with strings and a shape. Only one had a semblance of a heel. The soles were all but lost. If they weren't hand-me-downs, then Tim had been awfully hard on them. I was growing numb from the cold. Or maybe it was from thinking of the youngster's plight.

"Aren't you about to freeze?" I asked.

Wiping a runny nose with a tattered sleeve, Tim managed a slight smile as he looked up. His ice-blue eyes sparkled. His mouth was missing a baby tooth or two. "Aw, it ain't so bad," he shot back in his best tough guy voice. "Ya get used to it after a while."

"Yep," I thought. "Ya get used to a lot of things, if you have a mind to." I figured that Tim had to do a lot of "getting used to things." A few more questions and about thirty-five more feet of film brought the story up to speed for the time being.

Before you could say "Jack Frost," I was back in the Opel getting warm. Even the camera was trying to freeze up. The Germans did make a nice car heater. I wished I could get Tim into the unit for a small thaw. I watched as the line grew shorter. Kids came out the side door with boxes under their arms and fresh leather on their feet. A few danced as they tested their new acquisitions. Tim shared their joy the best he could. He gave them that toothless smile and the comment, "Look good on ya," as he admired their prizes. Mostly, he nodded and stomped his feet. He had warm thoughts. He would soon be them.

The line grew shorter and shorter as it disappeared into the church building. Then it stopped. I got out of the car, ready to film Tim getting his shoes. Now Tim was on the top step about to enter when the door opened and then closed in his puzzled face. I watched and my heart stopped. Then the door opened again, just wide enough for a face to announce, "No more shoes. We're out."

I was shocked. First I was jubilant that I got the announcement on sound. Beautiful! Then I recorded Tim's terrible disappointment. A different, sadder story was made. I was reeling at the cavalier attitude toward the one kid left. There were just too many youngsters but not enough shoes for the very last kid.

Now, a working newsman is not part of the story. I knew that. I had recorded the end of the great shoe giveaway. I had the final word: Tim's assertion that it "wasn't so bad." But Tim was two hours out in the freezing cold and had no new shoes. I told myself to remember that a newsman is not part of the story.

But I had to have another word from Tim. "Tell me how d'ya feel not getting any shoes?" I asked. Tim took another swipe at his runny nose with the other sleeve. "I think my sister got some shoes. I hope so. She really needed 'em."

The story was finished. I pulled out of the pockmarked parking lot. It was a good thing the ground was frozen or the Opel would have been buried in mud.

I glanced to my left as I turned onto Bernal Street. There was Tim, walking along with his hands in his jeans and his head bowed in thought. Recognizing me, he waved, with a big smile on his face. That smile. It was like, "No shoes—no big deal." Amazing! Was today like any other day for Tim? Disappointment after disappointment? Get used to it? Tim's young life must have been full of disappointments.

I did something I seldom did. I let my mind ponder the situation. I told myself that the troubles of others are to be left with them. Don't get involved because you could end up with a truckload of involvement. But as I spurred the German across the prairie to Fort Worth to get the story on the air, I couldn't help thinking what a brave little guy Tim turned out to be. It gave me a sad heart to think that there was nothing I could do to help the situation.

The story aired that evening at 10:00 p.m. on *The Texas News*. The phone rang off the wall the next day. It had made a lot of people sad. They wanted to help. The station facilitated the response, which turned out to be enormous. I used my investigative talents to find out what kind of shoes Tim really needed and wanted. The family, who lived in one of those thin houses, had other needs, too, which were met with the generosity of those who had caught the spirit of the season. Christmas was coming and so was Santa. It made a newsman's cold heart warm.

The Watering Hole

They were affectionately labeled "watering holes"—oases for the city's talented, hardworking news hawks. Places for a guy to give himself a liquid prize and maybe some nourishment after a long, hot day. The Joe Banks Restaurant, owned by Joe and Eva Banks, was just such a watering hole. But at 5:00 p.m., there was very little water. There was beer, lots of beer. Bourbon, too, if you brought your own. Neither Dallas nor Texas was a mixed-drink city, county or state.

When Dallas's newsmen beat their deadlines or finished their stories, they wanted to wind down and talk about their day, their stories or the accomplishments of other people. Mostly they wanted to talk and hear themselves talk. They loved to tell stories as much as they liked to write them.

So they gathered at watering holes like Joe Banks after the day was finished. They drank and talked. And laughed. And the more they drank, the more they laughed. They seldom gathered in bars. It didn't set well when the wife had to tell the children, "Your daddy is running a little late 'cause he's conducting business in a bar downtown." "He is at a meeting at a downtown restaurant" was more acceptable. And Joe Banks was a good one. Being a few steps from the courthouse, it was in great demand at lunchtime. Lawyers, court clerks, jurors and newsmen could always get a hot, cheap, tasty lunch plate quickly at Joe Banks.

I liked to chow down there. My addiction to cornbread was satisfied daily with a reliable supply, hot from the oven. The chili was the best anywhere up and down the Trinity Valley. Even Melvin Beli, who later loused up poor old Jack Ruby's murder case, praised Eva's red.

Now it was quitting time, and the dying sun was burying itself behind the Trinity River levee. Usually this time of day, the courthouse was spilling out its greatest asset: beautiful women. An errant breeze was now likely to send a hem sailing upward, Marilyn Monroe–style. It was always worth being in the vicinity of the house of justice at quitting time, just to witness some of Dallas's famous female beauty.

I looked both ways on Main Street as I neared the antiquated entrance to the old brick building housing Joe Banks. If you paid any attention to the ancient oak door, which might or might not shut behind you, or to the old stamped-tin ceilings bearing years of grease because they were too high to really clean or paint, you might be inclined to take your business elsewhere. But for me, this was lunch home.

The aroma of the fiery chili and the thinly battered fried chicken lingered faintly around the room. But the most prominent smell, the one that gave the room its distinctive ambience, was the smell of the cedar oil treatment that was applied regularly to the well-worn pine floor. Even if I were blindfolded, I would know I was in Banks.

My bunch was gathered around the big black table in a far corner of the room. The veteran newspapermen slumped over their drinks and sipped as they swapped stories about their days. The younger pups, the television and radio blokes, liked it best when the "old dogs" started barking about the good old days. Some of the tales told were beyond belief, but there was always another old-timer who remembered the incident and vouched for its validity. It probably cost the storyteller a beer.

The cacophony was like what you might find in a military barracks. Everyone is talking but no one can hear. The person who thinks he has the most important thing to say keeps raising his voice until he drowns out the less interesting talkers. Everyone then listens and waits his turn, thinking, "This story better be good." "Hi, Bert" may be the best or only greeting a newcomer gets, since the conversation never misses a beat.

"Beer, Mary," I shouted to a plump and tired but still smiling waitress, who knew I wanted a Pearl. But today Mary announced, "No Pearl. Sold 'em all to some other thirsty people. Man from the land of the sky blue waters oughta' be here tomorrow with some Hamm's Beer. How about a real cold Lone Star?" She paused, rolling her hands, smacking and winking. How could a fellow resist?

"Being it's you, you silver-tongued heifer, I'll take it," I smiled, getting a little eloquent. "You know you could sell lizard poop to a horse-dung peddler." Mary's lumberjack laugh hacked out from years of smoking Old Gold cigarettes.

Saul Crum from the *Morning News* sipped on some real liquor. Pat Ridgeway of **KBOX** radio nursed the last mug of suds he could mooch. They were listening intently as Terry O'Neal held forth. "I'm tellin' you, this story is honest-to-god true. It happened over in Arkansas one night when we were on a football trip. I got the only waitress within ten miles to bed down with me. We were way out in the boonies so the players could get some sleep. This cocktail waitress was the only skirt around there, and everyone was after her. Well, I got her. We were in my bed about to make out, and she said right out of the blue—right out of nowhere—"I wish my husband could see me right now."

"Your husband?!" Terry exaggerated his shocked reply. "Where the hell did you come up with a husband? Especially at a time like this!"

"Oh," the waitress smiled and cooed, "I'd like to make the SOB jealous to a serious degree. He is such crumb. Best he can do is a damned night watchman's job."

"Where?" Terry pretended interest while the business end of him was starting to lose power. "Where the hell is he going to be jealous?"

"He's pulling night duty right here at this motel," she said matter-of-factly.

"That did it!" Terry recalled, "She had no concern whatsoever. But it deboned my chicken for the whole night."

Switching from the glory stories of sexual exploits to more mundane subjects, Joe Dave Scott broke in as he sat down with his usual ice-cold Schlitz. He was seldom seen without it. "What's the word from the city?"

Bill Glad, metro reporter at the *Times Herald*, had just left the city council meeting. "It was hot. It was dull. It was long and drawn out," Glad said. "I left old Pat Conway there to make sure nothing went on that we didn't know about." Then, with an evil grin, he said, "We sure hung him out to dry today. Bet he is still fuming." Clearly, a story was coming.

"See, old Pat is hung over like a wet sheet on a high line. He put his head down on the press table, propped up by his arm. He was snoring before his next breath."

Now, news people do not have a funny bone in their bodies when it comes to the outside world invading their domain, but doing it to one another is always in order. Tricks on one another are only limited by imagination. City hall reporters were not usually the ones to do this, but today was hot and dull and Pat was hung over.

As Glen told it, the microphone in front of Councilwoman Elizabeth Blessing was moveable. Recognizing a chance to spark an otherwise dull afternoon, Glen asked her to hand it to him. She did. He placed the microphone down under Pat's arm, near his nose.

The volume was up, way up. Suddenly, the sound of Pat's snoring engulfed the council chamber. All of the council members were stunned. Where was the snoring coming from? The investigation didn't take long, because Glen helped, directing their attention to KBOX's talented reporter, Pat Conway. Then Glen announced to the council, "If you all don't liven things up, we all are going to konk out."

"Liven it up!" Mrs. Blessing shot back. "I think you just did!"

All of the council members laughed and went back to discussing city business, except the mayor. According to unnamed sources, he had gone to sleep even before Pat.

The day was winding down, and so were the stories. Jim Tickler, a Mississippian who could dip snuff, drink beer and chatter in his syrupy southern dialect all at the same time, was the *Times Herald*'s best courthouse reporter. He was thoughtful now. "Whatever happened to Jim Mixon? The only thing I heard was that he was found dead in his house. Not even much of a mention in the paper." The group was silent.

Then J.D. Renfroe said, "Never heard much about it. But the police seemed to think he choked to death. Too bad. He was a hell of a nice guy."

No one knew the end of that story. Newsmen who responded to the police scanner were shocked when they found that the victim was a friend and colleague.

"Seems like being in the reporting business can be hazardous to your health," said Bob Kindling. The group was quiet. Two reporters had been murdered. One general assignments reporter was killed at his house by what the police figured were probably seriously bigoted juveniles. An amusements writer was murdered and left in an Oak Cliff park.

"Aw, cut the crap," Stud Staples said, breaking the suddenly somber mood. "This is getting depressing. Man, I had a rough start today, but with the help of a Pearl or two, I'm gonna end it on a high note."

Mary checked bottles and glasses to see if she couldn't save some steps. The sun was about to drown in glorious red and orange in the Trinity River at the west end of Commerce. All of the courthouse beauties were probably home now, cooking dinner. A couple of leftover wannabe beauties were cackling two tables over, but they had baited their hooks for lawyers. It was rumored that mouthpieces had money—drink money. But no real funny stories to tell at Banks.

The Hangar Demolition
and then Ellie

It was not yet dawn. The sun hadn't cleared the modest dwellings, which looked like black cutouts against the pink sky over Elm Thicket, across Lemmon Avenue from Love Field.

To Slim Murray, WBAP's senior photographer, time was of the essence. When he realized that the old Braniff Airways maintenance hangar at Love Field was going to be dismantled, he had an idea for an offbeat film story. He was famous for such epics.

The four giant wooden girders that formed the skeleton for the huge, aging hangar were fifty feet high, seventy-five yards wide and the same distance from one another. Slim had learned that the contractor dismantling the old hangar was first going to remove the metal skin that covered the structure. Then, with a single cable, his crew would connect those four towering skeletal arches at their apex. The end of the cable would be connected to a vehicle—a little Ford tractor—that would pull the whole thing down. Slim had told me several months ago that he wanted to film the entire project.

This was the morning of "D" Day—Demolition Day. The metal skin on the hangar had been removed. Slim was more excited than he was when he discovered a three-legged dog that climbed a tree up in Fannin County. This time it was four huge arch-like beams that, when tugged, would provide a once-in-a-lifetime picture of a domino effect as one toppled earthward, dragging the others down in succession. This would be one girder crash deluxe.

I had been recruited to provide photography services with my Bell & Howell hand camera, with the speed set at sixty-four frames per second. Such an adjustment would provide slow-motion pictures when projected at twenty-four frames per second.

I discovered when I first signed on with Channel 5 that I could learn a lot by following Slim around. I considered this outing another of those worthwhile "follow-arounders."

The traffic along Lemmon Avenue was light at this early hour. An easy, cool breeze filled an orange canvas windsock on the peak of a nearby hangar. The breeze would likely not be a factor in this endeavor.

I received last-minute instructions from Slim, who appeared to have his plans thoroughly mapped out. He was sharply focused as he busied himself pacing, measuring the terrain, then the girders and then the terrain again. All appeared to be ready when Slim exuberantly hopped aboard the little tractor. Waving to me, he became the mock operator, pretending to start the whole operation.

At that moment, something went awry. The huge arches trembled. The lead girder on the south end appeared to respond to slack from an action initiated at the little tractor. Then Slim, realizing that something was badly wrong, leaped from the little tractor. The giant girder next in line was now pulling on its neighbor. From that point on, it was cataclysmic. Four big arches headed toward the ground. As a huge cloud of dust filled the hangar, the northernmost girder drew taut, its cable pulling a passenger: a flying Ford tractor. It flipped through the air like a tamale cart caught in a tornado, flinging parts everywhere as it gained altitude. As the fourth arch crashed to the ground, the little tractor was flung toward the street. It was truly a once-in-a-lifetime picture of a girder crash deluxe. I was shooting the whole thing as Slim came running full-speed past me. He crossed Lemmon on a dead run with his Cinevoice sound camera and tripod hoisted over his shoulder. Where his power battery could be was anyone's guess.

"Meet 'cha at the White House," he hollered, glancing toward Mockingbird Lane, where he saw the little tractor tangled in a chain link fence.

The neighborhood reverberated with the noise. A plane crashing into the Coca Cola plant on Mockingbird Lane would not have been louder. Naturally, the crash truck from the Love Field fire station pulled out with siren screaming. The firemen left their breakfast on the stove as they responded in emergency mode to the loud crash and then the huge dust cloud. Being only a few blocks away, they were charging through the smoke cloud, hoses spraying, only minutes later. When their adrenaline subsided, they scratched their heads and looked quizzically at one another. Instead of a raging fire, they had been tilting at a windmill. Only the dust of a huge demolition mess. Curiously, no one spoke a word. They just boarded their fire trucks and drove away. Breakfast was waiting.

The White House was a six-stool, five-table, four-booth greasy spoon diner in downtown Dallas. It was squashed up on a corner between a parking lot and a sidewalk mailbox at Field and Ross. The little cracker box structure was situated just a block north of the afternoon newspaper, but no one from the *Times Herald* with an ounce of self-respect wanted to be seen patronizing the place. Slim and I were patrons. I often gave the place my lunch business because I sorta' felt that when a newsperson wore Robert Hall suits and had his hair cut by a first-semester barber school student, he could not afford to be too proud.

The place usually had no waitresses. Most days at breakfast time, a customer would just shout an order to a beefy, loudmouthed fry cook with hairy, Popeye arms. Some of his usual customers whispered that his name was Clyde. Besides cooking, he supplied the humor that ricocheted off the grease-stained walls: "I'm chief cook and bottle washer, and if ya make me any trouble, I'm the owner."

For thirty-five cents, the White House offered a breakfast "Express Special." It consisted of two eggs and a serving of meat with toast and a cup of coffee. Not bad when it was served on a clean plate. But cleanliness was not always on the menu. In fact, regular patrons were known to request a glass of water, so when no one was looking, they could dip the utensils in the water and wipe off yesterday's gravy with a paper napkin.

I stepped into the café through the already open door. It was getting hot, despite the open window and the screen door providing ventilation. I found Slim at a back table giving a woman, apparently a waitress, a ration of early-morning crap—leftover anger from his disastrous Love

Field project. He had ordered his eggs over easy. Presumably, they were not to his liking, so he noisily suggested that she return them to "the oaf who thinks he is a chef."

The waitress, ignoring Slim, turned and looked at me as I slid into the booth with its worn, red plastic covering. "Excuse me," I apologized with what I hoped was a friendly smile. Whatever the reason she was here today, I thought, she was certainly a decorative addition to the place.

"What can I getcha?" asked the waitress, a look-alike for Keeley Smith of Louis Primo fame, with a dazzling smile. I couldn't resist a tired old cliché: "What's a lovely young thing like you doing in a dump like this?"

She responded with just a hint of seduction in her voice. "I'm just helping ole' Clyde out of his morning jam. You might say I'm unclogging his jam. I do other things in more, ah, commodious climes." She actually said "more commodious climes." One of her big brown eyes flipped a lazy, lash-laced wink.

"Come get Mr. Adolphus Hotel's uptown eggs and I'll let you relax. Thanks for your help!" Clyde shouted over the roar of a passing postal truck gunning it east on Ross.

I still hadn't caught her name as she set the plate of eggs before Slim for the second time. She looked expectantly at him, hoping to catch a gleam of satisfaction from a finicky diner. He grabbed his knife in one hand and fork in the other and chopped into the eggs as though they were a chunk of beef. Then he leaned against the back of the booth. Looking directly into the questioning eyes of the lady server, Slim flipped the plate, eggs and all, over on the table. "I said I wanted these over easy. Now they are over easy!"

The ugly mess was running all over the table when the waitress suddenly leveled her arm from the elbow to her wrist and swiped the entire mess into Slim's lap. "Now you snake-eyed egg-sucker, that's really over easy. You better hightail it outta here before somebody whips your finicky ass!" she yelled.

There was only a stunned silence from the three other diners in the place. The only noise came from Slim, who scooted out of the booth uttering a flurry of unintelligible expletives while trying to stem the slime of somewhat over easy eggs running down the front of his gray corduroy pants.

"Ya ain't gonna get a show like that here every morning," Clyde laughed fiendishly. Everyone else tittered nervously, except the waitress. Angrily, she was using a damp table rag to clean the egg off her arm. "Son-of-a-bitch," she growled. "How do I get myself in these messes?" She looked at me as if I could provide an answer.

"I haven't the slightest idea, sweetie," I said. "I know I've seen your face before, but your name escapes me something fierce."

"I don't imagine you do recall our last encounter. I'll get you another cup of coffee, and we can play twenty questions." She dipped her chin slightly and batted her eyes several times.

She brought a steaming coffee in one of those heavy white diner mugs. Then she snickered as she asked me if I would care for a plate of eggs. I gave her a quizzical look as she slid in beside me, purring, "Let me sit here. Somebody really messed up that other side. By the way, I'm Ellie. You may remember me as Ms. Lone Star. You were reporting, and I was—and still am—your favorite *Times Herald* switchboard operator. Make that your favorite, lonely switchboard operator."

I pounded the table lightly with a doubled-up fist, remembering back at least two years. "Sure, I recall that. I should have picked up on your voice. Everyone in the newsroom fell in love with your voice."

"Well, that's a useful new piece of news," Ms. Ellie cooed. "If I'd known that, I would have been a little more confident that time when I tried to hustle you into buying me a Lone Star." She caressed the words "Lone Star" just a little. She leaned over toward my right ear, balancing her approach with her hand on my leg. "I'd still like you to teach me how to suck the twinkle outta one of them cold Lone Stars. I hear it's never too late to learn, and I'm a real willin' pupil," she confided, almost whispering. I thought I felt her tongue flick by my right ear.

Movin' On

Never too organized, I was always too occupied with my day-to-day existence to set goals. Uneasy with the unseen and unknown, I never wanted to peek behind the curtain shielding an uncertain future. The truth was that I was a doer, not a planner. I just let life happen and then decided what to do or how to react to it. I had a good job and a good reputation as a reporter for WBAP-TV Channel 5. Up until then, my method, or lack of it, had worked. That all changed one night at Commerce Street and Beckley Avenue. I was offered a job.

It happened at a gruesome accident scene in the middle of the night at an elevated icehouse just a beer can's throw off Commerce at Beckley. A car occupied by two guys failed to make the Beckley curve and plowed head-on through some latticework and way up under the structure. They were what the police call a twenty-seven—dead at the scene. They would have been just banged up if their car had not run so far under the building. The hardtop vehicle, according to firemen, "was turned from a sedan into a convertible." The occupants lost their heads.

At that macabre scene, I was shocked to be approached by Houston Schneider, the news director at WFAA-TV Channel 8. He suggested that I come to work at WFAA in Dallas. And not just "work," but rather fill the job as his assistant news director. At that exact time, in that grisly setting, my future did flash before my mind. Assistant news director! My thoughts were tumbling wildly, hidden behind what I hoped was a cool, calm façade. I was uncomfortable having anyone see me either sweat or jump for joy.

Houston and his wife, Lou, were real wreck-runners, his wife especially. When the season was right, she would dress in her short shorts and show up at the scene with her camera. News guys loved it.

Despite the setting, the offer had been fermenting for some time. Lou was the one who let the cat out of the bag. She said that Houston couldn't sleep at night because he kept thinking about how I always seemed to be the first at a news scene. According to Lou, what drove Houston crazy was how I seemed to be in two places at once. Actually, I just had a system. I figured that if I couldn't make it to the crash scene before the ambulance loaded and left, I would hightail it to the emergency room entrance of the designated hospital. Pictures of a victim on a stretcher were a must. It made no difference where they were taken. Dripping, wrecked autos were essential but not much of a turn-on for the viewer who tuned in to see gore. Those crumpled vehicles weren't going anywhere anytime soon. They would be there for pictures when a photographer got there later.

Now if Big Tiny Little Junior, the black ambulance driver, was running a wreck, I could always count on beating him to the scene. Big Tiny Little Junior weighed in at about 320 pounds. His ambulance, no. 608, was always identifiable miles away because, under his weight, it listed mightily to the left. You could almost hear that tormented Chevrolet's springs scream for mercy when the driver settled in and started rolling.

No matter which direction the wreck scene was, B.T.L. Junior first circled by his girlfriend's house on Colonial Street, the ambulance swaying and the siren howling. If his girlfriend was out hanging a line of clothes, she'd give a slight wave in his direction. Nothing too enthusiastic. Some said the lady wasn't as thrilled about the noisy ambulance as Tiny Little Junior was. "Disturbed the whole neighborhood," she'd say.

The exploits of B.T.L. Junior were memorable. One time at Hall and Bryan Streets, he lost a body on a gurney from the back of his ambulance. He radioed the police dispatcher, "Do we need the ME if the victim has already expired? Oh, and send an accident investigator. The man on the stretcher done hit another car, too."

All that history notwithstanding, here in the middle of the night on an obscure end of Beckley Avenue, just before it turned into Canada Drive, I pondered the biggest offer of my life.

Houston had used up all of his film shooting the scene before the firemen extracted the auto from under the building. The best pictures were yet to come, like shots of the officers placing sheets over the bodies. Houston swore at his predicament. "No more film here or there or anywhere! Lou, you been shootin' it all up on some pissy-assed dog show!" Houston was an ex-marine with a short temper. He was thunder and lightning when he was unhappy.

Feeling a certain amount of compassion for him, I handed Houston my last roll of DuPont Tri-X. Houston was overcome, but not so much that he couldn't load his old Bolex there in the dark. He was out of light, too. I shared the beam off my Fritzo lamp.

Houston was ready when the bodies were loaded into the ambulance. "Can I come by your house tomorrow and talk?" Houston asked, as we stumbled through the night to our news units. Lou led the way, the wiggle of those white short shorts visible in the dim light of a streetlamp.

Houston's offer was a good one. The money was fair. And several perks, like medical insurance and a pension plan, seemed reasonable enough to entice my move from my lowly position in the Dallas bureau of WBAP.

Television was, as I figured it, an idea whose time had come. The book on TV news gathering was being written and rewritten every day. That's how I was lured out of the newspaper business in the first place. James Byron, a veteran newsman out of the *Fort Worth Star Telegram* stable, was hiring newspapermen, "real journalists," to replace the "button-pushers," as some called the guys who labored in the electronic media. They were to shoot a story, not just pictures. Writers like Russ Thornton, Tom McDonald and Clint Bourland were legendary with that technique at Channel 5. They could take any roughly shot film and make it a compelling piece to view on the famous *Texas News*. And that was the one big reason that I didn't want to leave. WBAP was the number one operation in the Southwest—maybe in the nation.

Now WBAP news director James Byron was not happy when I told him of my intentions. But he knew that with no advancements for me on the horizon, someone else would make an offer soon. The business was growing. Stealing talent was becoming as common as the innovations in the industry. Color was coming. I had already shot color film over in East Texas. Vividly colored dogwoods in bloom made it on the air one Sunday. I took the WFAA job as assistant news director.

On my first day at WFAA-TV, General Manager Mike Shapiro summoned me to his office to welcome me aboard. Then he gave me a surprise as big as Houston's offer of a job: he wanted to fire Houston Schneider right then and there. "I'm ready to fire that son-of-a-bitch here and now." Shapiro was serious as he looked me square in the eyes. I had to think fast. I needed to calm Shapiro down a little. I knew it wasn't right to kick the old marine out without at least a warning.

"Mr. Shapiro—Mike—what Houston needs now, more than firing, is some help, some assistance from a person who doesn't want his job. He needs loyalty. That bunch he has in the newsroom—there is not one that doesn't want his job—except for maybe that goofy journalism teacher from Irving who shoots football on the weekend."

Shapiro said that he had warned Houston several times about his temper and his lack of management skills. "Tell you what, my friend," he stared at me and pointed a rod of a finger. "One year from today we'll talk. If he doesn't make the grade with you behind him, he's done."

I walked down the hall back to the newsroom, wondering if Houston knew that he was walking a 365-day plank—if he knew that the only friend he had on the entire news staff was a schoolteacher from Irving who just wanted to shoot football...if he knew that his assistant news director might very well be taking his spot in a year.

I took my new responsibilities seriously, though I was uncomfortably aware that several of the staff resented my being brought in as assistant news director. I tried to run the news operation with an even hand.

It was a great time to be at WFAA-TV. Besides my new job, I loved the new television studio headquarters that the *Dallas Morning News* ("Big Daddy" to those who labored in the electronic media) built in 1961.

Actually, my love affair began when I did a story on the construction progress of the new building at 606 Young Street, right across the street from the *Dallas Morning News* headquarters. Through the last several months of building, I lovingly recorded on film every step in its progress. Finished now, the gleaming white building was located only a couple of miles from the station's antiquated quarters on Harry Hines but still a world away in its styling and equipment. The old building, with its musty smell and ancient equipment, was given to KERA, a most grateful public television station. According to WFAA-TV chief engineer Jim W. Cooper, the new TV and radio stations were years ahead of their time. They were state of the art, the best in the nation. Now it was an indescribable pleasure to walk the spacious halls and smell the "new" everywhere.

But as is true of every place but paradise, everything was not perfect just because the *building* was new and perfect. I often thought it was too bad that some of the old, dusty employees couldn't have been left in the old, dusty building.

WFAA-TV and Radio was a company as conservative as Ronald Reagan. It did not hold with highflying skirts or spirits. Employees were expected to be as buttoned-down as undertakers. But in the early '60s, a wild rash of crazy behavior seemed to have broken out in the whole country. WFAA-TV and Radio, long known for its stiff upper lip and staunch conservatism, caught the fever.

I had been assistant TV news director for only a few months when I became a little embarrassed by a couple of the uncouth occupants of the radio side of WFAA. Some deejays were actually caught in deep night spinning something besides records in one of the control rooms—in the company of some very willing "fans."

For a time, I rationalized that they were only radio people. What could you expect? They were not really my responsibility. But I felt personally humiliated again when they cooked up a batch of brownies laced with marijuana. Although, to be honest, a secretary was the actual chef. The radio staff people were the ones who carelessly "left" the tin pan with the naughty ingredient in an open space on a receptionist's desk. A prowling sales manager stalking his wayward charges spied the pan of fresh goodies. As was his nature, he snitched a bar or two.

It took two hours to peel the unsuspecting sales manager off his office wall. Some say that he looked like a motorcycle in a hippodrome, going around and around and spinning out. I figured that at least the experience taught him to keep his treat-snatching habits in check.

But the real mishap was bigger than those penny-ante pranks. For years, when some of the old employees gathered to tell old tales, the story about the Grinch who stole more than Christmas would come up.

It all began, appropriately, with television—a set, that is. Nationally, color television was becoming the new toy, the new status symbol. And around the early '60s, such sets were very hard to come by and very expensive. Manufacturers had not yet ramped up to provide at least one, often more than one, to every household in the country. But what a perfect Christmas gift for the man from "across the street," top man in the whole Belo empire: Joe Dealey, president of the *Dallas Morning News* and WFAA-TV and Radio. The television set as a present was the inspiration of WFAA-TV manager Mike Shapiro, who was himself turning heads across the nation with his management techniques. A wise fellow, indeed.

Mike and I decided that we would choose and buy Joe Dealey's Christmas present: a giant, state-of-the-art color television set, the kind that, at that particular time, you could not buy for love or money. But Shapiro's clout came through. It was delivered late in the fall in a big wooden crate. It was really big. It had to be stored in the far back area of the building, where props and other unused stuff were stored. The crate rested there, unnoticed, for weeks before the Christmas season.

When the morning arrived to give Joe Dealey his Christmas present, all station personnel were present. Ladies tittered. Men cleared their throats. Everyone was anticipating the opening of that big box. Mike spoke appropriate words, sprinkled with the usual platitudes. Then a little crane was hitched to the really big crate. The moment had arrived. Someone started the engine on the little machine. It whirred and the ropes grew taut. A secretary in the back row, near the set of the children's program *The Peppermint Show*, giggled with excitement. The big crate was slowly raised into the air. But nothing appeared from under the crate. The pallet was bare. Something had gone wrong, badly wrong. Where was the giant, state-of-the-art color television set?

A couple of engineers wisely stifled laughter that could have been heard back at union headquarters. The secretaries were open-mouthed and totally silent. Mr. Dealey appeared to choke, but his normally red face remained normal and red.

I never thought I would see anyone breathing fire, but Shapiro snorted flames. The employees who were present vowed to never again position themselves to face such rage. Incredibly, the television set was never found. The culprit who managed to steal it was never discovered. In the weeks that followed, I never dreamed that an occasion would ever again arise to equal the Dealey Christmas catastrophe. But it did.

State highway patrolman John Poor always strolled into the newsroom when he came to deliver the Department of Public Safety (DPS) safety videotapes, which the station ran as public service announcements. But one day, with his big, off-white Stetson in place atop his size seven-and-a-half head, he motioned to me to follow him to the break room, where we were securely alone. John wanted to divulge what he called a "rock-knocker."

He whispered, "I'll get right to it. There are some pretty bad people out there making some mighty filthy movies. I think they call 'em pornographic. We're gonna stop 'em." John continued, looking around to make certain that my ear was the only one he was bending. "We have some undercover investigators who got in with this porn bunch. They got lots of documentation for a raid."

I was all ears now, thinking that a crackerjack news story might be in the making—a lightning-like raid and the subsequent arrests of sleazy women, as well as scum-ball-ugly men. I could see it all now. John could see the road I was traveling. He paused. "Bert, I'd rather clean an outhouse full of black widow spiders than have to tell you that at least one of your men is involved."

I gasped. "Who is involved and how?" I was almost shouting. John shushed me, anxious that no one else could hear.

"The investigators found out that the camera used to shoot the doing and screwing was from Channel 8. It had the big Circle 8 decal on the side. But," John said, "as if that isn't enough, all that film is being developed in your processing machine."

I felt sick. What the hell was somebody thinking? "Who was it?" I asked, afraid of the answer. When John told me, I was more than angry. "That son-of-a-bitch! That holier-than-thou bastard!" The offender was, to his coworkers, a professed Christian type of guy. Now I was about to lose my religion. "Well, is that the worst of it?" I dreaded the answer.

"That's about it," John said. "I just wanted you to get your side cleaned up before we really cracked down. I, we, the DPS, owe you and Channel 8 a lot. That's why we're telling you about it." Another pause. "I don't want to have to tell the story twice, so who's at the top of the ladder—the guy who's going to have to do the dirty work?" John was serious.

Mike Shapiro came immediately to my mind. He was the top rung on the broadcast ladder. In good times he got the glory, and when things went awry he took the heat. Of course he must be told. But Mike would be livid. He would go through the roof. The more I thought about it, the more I was overcome with fear. I had seen the explosive extent of that Shapiro temper. Best get it over with before a heart attack set in. "How much time do we have?" I asked.

It was then nearly 10:00 a.m., and folks were starting to trickle in for the morning coffee break. I was thinking as fast as I could about the best way to tell Mike. It had to be good, and right the first time. Damn! I wished Shapiro was out of town and Jim Pratt was in charge. Jim was funny. He might even laugh before he went to pieces. I was sure that Mike wouldn't laugh.

Later in my office, with a gut feeling like a loose bag of pecan shells, I nervously dialed Mike's extension. Got Velma Collins, of course. I liked her. Never hid her thoughts. "Velma, Bert here." She always said she knew my New Mexico voice. "I need to talk with the man. The mister man…today," I said, choking a little.

Knowing Mike's schedule to the second, Velma told me to come on up. I had forgotten to tell her that a DPS officer was with me. Velma blinked at the officer's unexpected appearance but swallowed hard and remained cool. She ushered us into Mike's big, comfortable walnut and leather office.

John told the story. Shapiro listened with pen and paper at hand, never taking a note. But he did seem to be taking it well. Then his complexion changed from its usual West Texas gopher tan to Canadian snow goose white. He slammed his pen down on his desk real hard. His jaw tightened; his steel eyes shot fire. "Okay, Beetle Bomb [that's what he called me, though he never explained why]. What's next?"

The officer told Mike how the raid was going to be staged. He said that it would be best if WFAA equipment was not covering the action

116

tomorrow night. It began to appear to me that the station might just jump through the fiery hoop and not get burned.

Shapiro wanted to know if I had anything else on my mind. I could only answer, "You can sure bet our camera equipment will be busy filming a church service somewhere. Wednesday is prayer meetin' night, ya know." Mike didn't find it very funny.

I charged on, saying that I thought Shapiro himself should handle the firing of the lab technician. "And if the DPS is going to let us off the hook, very few people will know about this. Best that the word doesn't get down to the pool hall or up to the Belo ivory tower."

The next day and night went off without a hitch. A surprised developer-photographer was sent packing. Channel 8 did not cover the raid and arrest. Actually, no one did. It was a surprise to every television station in the city.

A day or two later, I met Shapiro in the hall. We exchanged "Good mornings," and Mike said that he wanted me to appear on his *Let Me Speak to the Manager* show. "We tape at 2:00 p.m. tomorrow. I want you there to explain why we cover so many car wrecks." He didn't crack a smile. I did. I loved him.

Minding the Store

I was never a hot shower fan. Semi-cold was more to my taste. It was 6:00 a.m., and hot or cold, this shower was hardly worth the name. It was just a skinny stream of water in a seldom-used company restroom shower. Trying to find the right combination of knobs to get the water just right was like trying to figure out bank safe tumblers.

I was cleaning up at the television station after one of the strangest nights in my news life. I had responded to a midnight fire call with "people in water." Police dispatches carried the incident as "cars in creek." A cloudburst in far North Dallas had turned the usually timid little Bachman Creek into a raging torrent. A wall of water had come cascading down on four cars moving both east and west on Northwest Highway. They were washed down the draw by the mad current and forced into the creek.

It was a big story that so much rain had fallen in such a short while. But the fact that eight people drowned in the blink of an eye was mind-boggling. Get this: the 11:45 p.m. "wall of wet death" simply wiped out four couples. One pair had to be pried apart from their "wet death-hold." I was on my way and was already writing the story.

It took until dawn for all four cars to be located and hauled out and bodies identified. I was in the creek the whole time. My Fritzo light was, for the most part, the only illumination. Lots of pajama-clad spectators who had to be evacuated from their luxurious creek-bank dwellings helped in the search. One was Bill Thurman, the movie guy who played the coach in *The Last Picture Show*. He turned out to be a real bloodhound when it came to spotting cars and bodies. Then he was named "rescuer of the night" when he produced a cooler of cold beer.

Now, in the early morning light, I really needed that shower before the news department meeting, scheduled for 7:00 a.m. Mike Shapiro accepted no excuses for not being there. I was assistant news director, and my boss was out of town.

Now, everyone who has been in the news business any length of time knows to stash a change of clothes somewhere. Getting your duds soiled happens when you least expect it. But unfortunately, on this particular day, I had no such stash to match my agenda. It was my first day as "news boss," the "in charge" guy, but I had no "in charge" clothes. And the department meeting was in ten minutes.

Then I remembered that the sportscaster had, in a newsroom closet, a week's worth of show threads, straight off the high-priced rack at a popular men's store. Naturally, the clothes were off-limits to all but the sports guy. But I was in no mood or condition to pay attention to that. I chose a jacket that passably fit. The sportscaster was admittedly a little thinner and his taste in clothes a little more flamboyant than mine, but I thought, "What the hell!" It was better than my wet, smelly clothes.

A few minutes later, as I headed for the front office conference room in my loud, tight clothes, I got wind of my need for a swish of deodorant. In a quick detour to the executive washroom, I employed an old standby measure: Juicy Fruit gum peeled halfway, with tinfoil still showing. Slip a piece of gum under the armpits. It's hell coming off, but in a pinch it cuts the stench.

All of the seats around the boardroom meeting table were filled, except for the one next to General Manager Mike Shapiro. I took it. Being this close to "the top," I was glad I had found that almost-forgotten toothbrush in the film compartment of my camera bag. It looked as though it had been used to brush out film flakes, but at least, with some hand soap from the bathroom dispenser, the bristles whisked away the death and decay of the previous evening.

The meeting did not begin on a good note. "Take off that lousy, loud jacket," Shapiro commanded. "Looks like something some sportscaster from Podunk would wear."

I slipped off the yellow-and-blue jacket. My arms, now in a short-sleeved shirt, exposed a cheap tattoo of a Mexican dagger. I hoped that Shapiro wouldn't notice the arm artwork or take note of my Hush Puppy shoes, still a little sloshy and getting gamey. For a fact, he could not tolerate one of his department heads flashing a tattoo.

Naturally, my tattooed forearm was the feature that drew the stares, grimaces and finally the comment, "How about that coat again. Let's see how it looks on you. Might be just right for a sport like you." Shapiro just grunted.

The meeting went off without a hitch. Department heads with no big agendas usually had short reports. Those with gain and glory in mind usually saved their crowing 'til they had the manager's ear in private. To be sure, the others didn't want to hear a lot of braggin' and boastin'. The finance officer did wonder if I had another piece of that Juicy Fruit gum.

Afterward, back in the newsroom, I slid into my chair behind the one thing that showed I wasn't "just another newsman." My desk displayed a plate with "Bert Shipp, Assistant News Director" stamped on it. I was proud of it.

The phone rang. "Bert, we miss your coverage over here at Commissioners Court. You always did a good job, especially when you were over at the *Times Herald*, where you had room to write. This abbreviated television time and space really crimps a reporter's style, doesn't it?" It was a commissioner on the county court.

"Yeah, Commissioner, you sure got that right. Coulda' written a book on 'No Time for Commissioners' when I switched from news rags to TV. But I'll bet you a mile of county road work that ain't why you're callin' me this time of year. Usually it's at Christmastime, when you need funds for your foster home kids, right?"

"Right, Bert. So right. But this time it's not that easy to discuss or, uh, talk about. But we heard your news director is out of town, and we knew we could hit you with a rather delicate matter. And I'll get right to it, Bert," he said. "You know how much we commissioners like the reporter covering the court now. She is a fair reporter, and she really don't make much trouble for you or us. You know how lots of reporters try to make a name for themselves. This lady ain't like that. She just sits at the press table, looks cute, takes notes, squirms and wiggles and, like I say, looks real good."

"Where the hell is he going with this?" I was mentally guessing, so I would have an answer when the time came. I had no clue where this commissioner was going.

He was really uncomfortable. "See, Bert, it's that fidgeting and squirming. Nothing wrong with crossing and uncrossing your legs. Gets ya comfortable. Do it all the time myself. But Bert, here's the rub. She's driving us crazy. Even old guys like Lawthon and Tiber are snortin' over it."

"Oh?" I grunted curiously. "Do tell. I can't wait to see where this is going."

The commissioner continued. "I don't know if you know it or not, but your reporter don't wear any panties. And I guess if she didn't have the second-prettiest pair of legs in downtown Dallas, we could kinda ignore it. As it is, we gotta have some relief. Can you help us?"

After having been up all night, I didn't have the strength to hold back uncontrollable laughter. I did muffle it, but finally the guffaws spilled over the line. "So who has the first-prettiest pair of legs in downtown Dallas?" I snickered and burst out laughing again. "Your secretary?"

"Bert, when you get through having fun with this, please help us. I'll be a real hero over here if this gets taken care of. [A pause] I know she's been here since April, and this is the first we've said anything. Don't ask me why it took so long to decide we'd had enough. Six months is only half a year." He snickered.

I just shook my head. I promised to do something, but what to do was something I would think about tomorrow. By now I really needed something to bring me back to reality. Just as I cradled the phone, "reality" sauntered regally in the door. "I see you're all the way back from Italy," I said, matching the superior attitude of reporter Jess Brown. "Thought you might talk some of your Catholic friends into getting you a job with the Pope. You were pretty high on their hog list." The air was thick with sarcasm.

Jess had talked the Cistercian monks running the University of Dallas into letting him do a story on the branch university they were starting in Rome. The university authorities then convinced Channel 8's news director to send Mr. Brown to do an "inside" story on the University of Dallas Junior Year in Rome—"the Italian study." And no one short of old Jess could handle the story as well.

But upon his return, Jess pushed his luck too far. "Just so you or the news director won't get bent out of shape when you see my time sheet and expense account, I thought I'd better caution you. There may be some surprises," he said. And surprises there were. His "work clock" as recorded in his time sheets started the moment the plane took off from Dallas. It continued to run, day and night, for five days until his aircraft touched the asphalt at Love Field again.

Asked why he chose to stay "on the clock" for the entire junket, he stuck his nose in the air and responded, "Hey, it was all your idea. I could've stayed home and saved your stingy asses a bundle. But if you choose not to respond appropriately to my request for reimbursement, the next voice you hear will be that of a lawyer…By the way, I walked so much I wore out a pair of shoes. These Italian alligators would have cost the station twice as much if I had bought them here."

Any other more sophisticated and experienced assistant news director would have said, "Thank you, Jess. We'll discuss this later when you have more time." I just fired Jess Brown right then and there. Apparently, job hunting had been in Brown's plans for some time. He did have another job a few months later.

At that point, it was only halfway through the day, and I was terminally tired. I looked out across the newsroom. The place looked like recess in elementary school. Talking, laughing, playing and pinching. I figured that the only thing that kept this place afloat was that the audience has no clue who is gathering news and how.

A wreck film here. Some city council meeting there. How about a nice Kiwanis luncheon? Don't forget the movie star who has arrived to promote her newest picture. Pack that in eight minutes. Give weather a few minutes to point around. And shove sports into what's left. That was probably what the viewers tuned in to see anyway.

No wonder there were few serious reporters on the staff and none in the wings. Most of them had wanted to be newspaper people. As *Dallas Morning News* editor Jack Krueger once told me, "Your TV bunch is just journalistically immature. Some day, when you can afford real reporters, y'all will grow up." I was a little put out by his frankness, but I knew Jack was right.

It wasn't really my problem—not just yet. I wasn't the news director. But I couldn't help wondering where this television news was going. Krueger's words haunted me. The whole Channel 8 bunch was immature.

It was like watching a West Texas farm crop. It sprouted and then waited for rain in order to grow. If no rain fell, the crop died. If television journalism didn't get some monetary nourishment, the field could not grow. And young, immature reporters would not stay long enough to mature into excellence. Old newsmen like James Byron over at WBAP and a few veteran TV news bosses also worried about it. "Until TV news operations get the bucks, the industry won't attract and keep really great talent." "Money is the rain our business needs" was often the opinion expressed at conventions and press club gatherings in late-night circles.

"Money is coming," the sages tried to convince one another, "but will we be there for the harvest?" The kids were coming out of journalism schools that printed pretty brochures showing Walter Cronkite's picture on the front. "You, too, can be a television news star," the booklets would tease.

Kids were graduating full of ambition and a sense of obligation because Pop had spent the family egg money to educate them. The world now owed them a place and a living. The spirit was willing, but the head was empty. They had to be taught all over again, if and when they did land a job in a newsroom.

Before the news director returned from his sabbatical, I crashed into one of the young, new-wave television journalists. Mike Shapiro had lots of acquaintances who had children wanting jobs in television. Ronnie Kleinfelder, the product of one such an unfortunate family, was now working at Channel 8. The kid was out of college without much direction or focus. He was not real crazy about much of anything but didn't think he should be doing any grunt work.

Ronnie had been around the WFAA-TV newsroom for a while. Never made a lot of waves. He wasn't real cooperative, but wasn't a troublemaker, either. In short, he was a mostly a slug to whom the world owed a living. But today was the wrong day to challenge my authority. He said no to a suggestion I offered about a nighttime assignment at the school building.

"You are not my boss," Ronnie snapped, pooching out his lower lip as he emphasized his discontent. It shocked me, but I'd had enough.

"Follow me, Ronnie, I want to show you something back here," I ordered, urging Ronnie toward a still photography darkroom. With the door slammed shut, in the thick darkness, I grabbed Ronnie by the tie. I rotated him around the tiny room, making certain he collided with every corner. "I'm not going to kill you, but you are going to think I am before you leave this place. You can get out of here alive when you grow up and decide there is someone on this earth here besides your little fat ass. Your big butt needs a lot of getting up off of!"

I was huffing and puffing. The overnighter, the commissioners' "no panties" problem and Jess Brown were catching up with me. I was ready to strangle Ronnie with his own tie. Fortunately, I remembered that this was Shapiro's friend's kid. Enough may have been too much. I flipped on the light. "Straighten your clothes and whatever is inside ya. Get over to the school building—*now*! And if you tell your parents about this, I will tell them exactly what happened."

Years later, when I was the old news director, the phone rang. "Mr. Shipp? WFAA television?"

"Yes. Shipp here. WFAA Television News."

"Hold the line for a call from Detroit please," the female voice said in her best professional manner. "You bet," I responded.

"Bert," the cultured male voice from Detroit boomed over the line many states away. "Ronnie Kleinfelder here. Remember me? You wiped up that darkroom with me one afternoon. I thought you were going to kill me. Scared the lazy, good-for-nothing hell out of me, you did. Do you remember that?"

"Who the hell did you say this was?" I asked. Then, memory came rushing back. "You bet I remember that day. Thought I'd probably lost my job for certain. How the hell are you? Haven't heard from you since then. What's been goin' on in your life?"

"Well, after that drubbing, I was too ashamed to stay at WFAA, and I had already applied at another place. I needed some time off to think about the 'necktie party' speech you made. I grew up in that darkroom that day. Mama and Daddy could not have helped me. Matter of fact, they should have taken me out to some darkroom and read me the riot act much earlier."

"Shucks, Ronnie, you make it sound like a classic, life-changing experience," I said.

"I want to thank you for helping me grow up. I owe you a lot. I never thought I'd get the chance to thank you," Ronnie added.

"Well, what are you doing up in Detroit now? That's the home of my favorite baseball team."

"I'm vice president in charge of Ford Motor Company's Public Relations Department. Come on up, and I'll let you use our box."

"Thanks." I smiled as I hung up the phone.

Best Interview

The Beatles

Most newsmen had plans for their lives. They knew where they were going and how they were going to get there. Planning and working their course, they scratched their future on bits of used news copy paper in the drawer and left them where they dumped their pocket contents every night. I wasn't much of a long-term planner. I mostly worked from one news event to the next, from one payday to the next.

Actually, if the truth were known, I became a news hawk by accident. I was studying to be an English teacher when I realized that, in the long run, I really needed to make a living. That drove me to look for a job with a newspaper. I thought I would never get the big prize or make the journalism hall of fame, but I would eat. Besides, what event could possibly happen that would catapult me to fame? The answer came from across the pond, from four Brits in whom I had no interest. Hell, I didn't even know one from the other.

The year 1964 went down in Dallas history as the year of the Beatles. They invaded America, landing in New York in September and then migrating across the country. Dallas developed a severe case of Beatlemania since Big D was to be honored with one of their stops. The closer the foursome got to the Southwest, the more fervent the interest became.

The intensity of the excitement caused even staid news people to do crazy things. The day before the "Fab Four" arrived, my boss had the harebrained idea to feed the furor that was building across the city. The idea was to do a preview of everything the Beatles would be doing. Braniff Airlines was bringing them in on a charter flight. So, complete with Beatle wigs, I went with three of my colleagues—Walt Stewart, Bob Walker and Dave Mulherne, grown-ups all—and talked the Braniff promotions woman into rolling the charter plane out of its preflight moorings onto the tarmac. There we four would-be Beatles tripped and dipped down the boarding stairs, acting like clowns for the rolling cameras. It wasn't much, but such a cornball story on TV would feed the fans until the real product made it to the local stage.

From the airport, our phony foursome was chauffeured in a limousine to the Cabana Motor Hotel on Stemmons Freeway. On a waiting red carpet, we were greeted by a bowing, scraping manager who played along with the gag. He said he needed the publicity. Sure he did. He would have the genuine articles the following day with plenty of publicity! Our faux four then frolicked in room 512, lighting smokes with the book matches that became souvenirs and flopping around in the beds where Ringo, Paul, John and George would be sleeping in just twenty-four hours. The make-believe arrival and staged hotel visit made it on the 6:00 p.m. news. The audience probably didn't care one way or another, but it was a hit with the newsmen's kids.

The next day, the Beatles made it into the city with the fanfare and insanity that was expected. Little girls went crazy at the airport. Their mamas joined in at the hotel. Despite all of this, the lads apparently spent a restful night.

A press conference had been planned to precede the Beatles' concert at the Convention Center on Friday night. All of the newsmen and cameras were gathered and set up for this most anticipated meeting in a room off the stage area.

I set up my camera and then went exploring the rest of the Convention Center. Not being too familiar with this area of the center, I was anxious to familiarize myself with the present surroundings. A dressing room there, a backstage entrance over there. I noticed another dressing room where a cop was standing. A cop? Standing? He wasn't standing, he was guarding! Maybe he was guarding the door of the second dressing room because some very important people might be in there?

I sniffed and cleared my throat as I walked toward the door where the policeman stood watch. I knew most of the officers on the force. This guy was familiar, a Hispanic guy named Pedro Rodriguez. I had seen him before, several times. "Que pasa?" I inquired in my best New Mexico Spanish. At the same time, I pushed the door open with surprising ease.

"Can't go in there," the cop said, astonished that someone would walk right in. "I'll get your daughter an autograph, Officer Rodriguez," I answered confidently. By this time, I was inside a dressing room I had been in many times before, especially on Golden Gloves fight nights. But no one was there. "Anybody home?" I shouted. My voice echoed off a wall of mirrors and across a concrete floor. "Is this place empty?"

The silence was disturbed then by the sound of shuffling feet. Like overgrown puppies racing from a backyard to greet a guest, here came "the boys," the Beatles, at least three of them. I couldn't tell which one was missing.

My apprehension about invading the Beatles' dressing room lasted only seconds. Incredibly, no one said, "What are you doing in here?" or "Get out. You don't belong here!"

Instead, I was stunned by their greeting. "Hey, Tex, what brings you in here? You sound like you're from Texas. Are you from Texas?" Ringo's accent was clipped, pure Liverpool, friendly and inviting.

Well, if it was Texas talk the boy wanted, talking Texas it would be, I thought, even if I had lived most of my life in New Mexico. I boosted myself up onto the dressing table, feeling the heat of dozens of light bulbs surrounding the giant mirrors. The three Beatles joined me.

"You guys like Texas?" I asked, nodding toward Paul, who was sporting the largest ten-gallon hat sold in or near cattle county.

"Got in late last night. Saw lots of lights from the plane."

"Lots of girls on the ground."

"No cowboys or cows."

"No guns either."

They took turns offering opinions but never stepped on another's line.

"Guess we won't get to see much of Texas. And we were really hoping to see lots of your West," Ringo said sadly. The only West they were going to get was what they could see from under those god-awful cowboy hats they were given at the airport. They did seem most grateful to get them. These guys were really nice—courteous, too.

"Where's the other guy?" I asked, trying to keep the conversation going.

"Oh, George? He had a rough night. Too much of something," Ringo supplied in the Queen's English. Then George appeared from wherever he had been hiding earlier. He did look like he might have had "too much of something," but it did not keep him from extending a hand. He joined the others on the dressing table.

Wanting to keep the conversation going, I kept asking questions. "Did y'all get hurt trying to fight off that mob when you got to the hotel? John, you look like you got hit. Are any of you writing a book? What kind of girls do you like?"

Amazed at my good luck getting a one-on-one interview, I realized that these gentlemen were letting me invade their sanctuary because I broke the monotony that resulted from their well-guarded lives. They saw no one but their handlers. They ate in their rooms. They appeared at news conferences. But no time was scheduled to let them get to know the real United States of America.

After a few minutes, I slipped out and hustled my sound camera into the dressing room. Then recording the answers to my questions was easy. Once I got careless and dropped my "Texas" accent. Ringo was quick to pick up on the slip. "Keep talking that Texas," he insisted.

When Ringo picked up a sack of Bull Durham and made an incompetent attempt to construct a "roll your own" cigarette, I showed him how it was done in Texas. A quick study, that drummer boy made his look like a ready-roll, even if it did look like one that had spent the night in a shirt pocket. Not bad, though, for a guy who had never tried to roll a smoke in a twenty-mile-per-hour wind atop a slow-moving horse.

George said that he was working on a book but didn't know the title 'cause "it wasn't written yet." John told of getting "punched in me face" as they fought their way into the Cabana Hotel last evening. The question about what kind of girls they liked evoked one answer from someone who mused that he liked John's wife. The conversation went on for at least fifteen minutes.

Afterward, as I walked my gear past the hoard of news people waiting to shout their questions, I just skipped joining the press conference and setting up all my equipment again. I wasn't certain just what I had, but I knew that I had an original Beatles interview and that I was the only one who did.

Years later, on occasions when I was introduced or given some acclaim, I was never cited for my coverage in Vietnam or Laos or for my work during the assassination, hurricanes or big crime cases. No, I was usually introduced as the reporter who slipped into the Beatles' dressing room and spent fifteen minutes in the company of the "Fab Four," who loved to hear Texas talk.

Chasing Missiles

L ate one afternoon, I found myself trapped in a time warp as I churned my way west on Lovers Lane from Preston Road. This once lovely North Dallas trail, formerly known as the Miracle Mile, was now just an urban artery, clogged bumper-to-butt with smoke-belching diesel Mercedes and Beamers. In this tangle, I was looking for a particular watering hole, a bar where a friend said to meet him. The daylight shining on the storefronts was slowly failing in a beautiful sunset.

"Ah, there it is." I breathed easier as I spotted the out-of-the-way drinking joint. A parking spot right in front was fortuitous. My bright orange news car looked psychedelic in the manufactured light from the surrounding shops—eerie but interesting.

I stepped inside what seemed to be a dark cave. After fishing around in my pocket, I came up with my last wooden kitchen match. The phosphorus came alive when I raked my thumbnail across its red-and-white head. I fired up a Salem cigarette and waited for my eyes to adjust to the darkness. The drone of the patrons' mumbling furnished another dimension to this black hole. Light from the Budweiser sign behind the bar blinked and buzzed. A spark was jumping a gap like it had a short. The bright, lavender Pearl beer light was more useful as I glanced down the line of butts that lopped over the bar stools. One of them might belong to my contact, who was actually an old acquaintance.

The butt with the hump in the back pocket was most likely my man. Private Investigator Joe Drum often had valuable information to pass along. He always "packed a rod"—at least one. Joe appeared to be watching the Bud sign, counting the times the short caused it to flicker. His ball-round face and styled, coal-black hair made him "quite good-looking," so said the ladies.

I found an empty stool next to Joe, who acted like he didn't see me. I gave him a bump with my shoulder. He flashed a clinched-jaw glance and faked a fist. I faked a grab for Joe's hip hump where the gun was resting. We both grinned.

"What ya say, Scout?" Joe offered, tilting a glass of Coca-Cola to his lips.

"Not much, Soldier." I tapped on the well-wiped bar for the bartender's attention. The professional backyard law enforcement–like talk meant nothing but acknowledged everything.

I knew Joe had just wrapped up a real dime-novel caper, closing the books on a big international art theft bust. A federal officer told me in confidence that Joe picked up $50,000 for rolling the thieves over. Before that, he had brought a bunch of gun smugglers to justice. He was just what the legitimate lawmen loved. He could start, do or finish a job that might be just outside the legal limits of a true law enforcement operation. He was a soldier of fortune—the best!

"How's bidness?" Joe inquired, not really serious with his question. He asked it to set up what was really on his mind.

"Bidness? Well, the last we had was pretty good." I played the game. "Ya know, news calves can't even get a squirt off a government tit. Heck, we can't even get close to the cow. Seems a bunch of P-I bulls have udderly taken over the pasture."

"You silly shit," the investigator said straight into my face. "If I didn't want to give you the drop on something you really need to know, I wouldn't put up with that crap from your deranged mind." The talk was a bit loud. The bartender frowned as he banged a frosty Pearl down on a Budweiser coaster. He watched for signs of possible violence. Joe and I broke into chuckles. No one on a bar stool laughs big, out-loud laughs. A chuckle is okay.

"Whatcha got for me that will make me famous and rich?" I asked, taking a long swig of a real cold Pearl.

"You ain't gonna believe this," Joe began. He told of a man who was the mayor of a tiny town in far West Texas. The guy was ambitious. He was also an entrepreneur, a farmer, a feed dealer and a real estate magnate. "It just goes on and on," Joe said, running his hand through his thick black hair.

I hadn't known Joe for long, but I could detect an air of real seriousness. The guy was really anxious to tell me something that he had found out. It sounded interesting. I scooted a little closer so I could get a better listen. "Keep talking. I'm rolling." I like to think that a clever newsman has a mind like a tape recorder. Joe went on to tell how this wealthy "farmer" got into the salvage business. It wasn't long before he found out about the juicy fruits of military salvage. The government barely gets a project budgeted and manufactured when it is, by certain design, "obsolete." That's when the salvage scavengers quit circling and land.

"Our farmer hero," Joe said, "bid on and won a guided missile system which went up for auction at Fort Sill, Oklahoma. Now get this," he continued excitedly. "This is a big, really big, thing. This thing he won guides missiles in the air. It's got computer cabinets, motors, dials and dishes. It's huge—a ton of merchandise!"

"I getcha," I followed, a little less interested, until Joe said, "He sneaked the son-of-a-bitch out of Fort Sill without it being demilitarized. He paid someone not to smash the good stuff. The shit that makes it work is still good. It's operational." He was on a high roll now. I listened now. We both reordered.

"Now get this," the detective gestured with outstretched hands waving. "This dude got word to me that he wanted to sell the system to a foreign country—Haiti or Chile, or to some crazy bastard with too much cash." He went on. "I struck a deal with him and made a couple of l-o-n-g trips to scope out what he thought was his market. I took a few bucks of front money off him and told him straight out that he was peeing in the wind. The market for guided missile systems was dead. He was not pleased. He wanted his front money back. I told him that, for a businessman, his hindsight was like the north end of a southbound mule."

Joe described how mad and hostile the dealer got. Even got to where he said that "I might 'be involved' in an accident." Oh boy! He shouldn't have crossed that line. "I don't think he's got the huevos to back up such a threat," Joe said. Then he explained that the more he thought about the whole deal the more aggravated he got. "I just thought I'd like to bring the son-of-a-bitch down, way down, like putting his ass in jail. I thought of exposing him. And, by golly, what better way than on a front page. Ya got any buddies in the paper business?"

"Well thank you, Mr. Drum." I considered Joe's proposal seriously. "How about some television exposure?" I raised my chin and snapped a quick sip of beer.

Joe continued. "How about you and that newspaper woman, the good-looking one over at the *Times Herald*—Martha something—trottin' out to the high plains and rippin' that sorry-ass operation apart? That mother missile is stashed in a Quonset hut on the edge of town. Easy to get at. What it'll cost you? How about the price of a burger and a bed?" He insisted. "I like the town of Lubbock 'cept when that friggin' wind howls. We could hole up there for the night. Whatcha say?" During the long pause that followed, I stared at Joe, studying his expressionless face. He stared back. Neither of us blinked.

I drained my Pearl as I swung my feet to the floor. I considered his proposal. "Hell of a story," I said. Thanks for the drop. I got a bunch a thinking to do on this one." As I brushed past the gallery of bar stool butts, Joe wheeled around on his seat and pitched a parting word: "Like to hear on this soon. And ain't her name MacAnally?"

Leaving the bar, I circled the last row of parked cars and saw Drum in the next lane. I eased to a stop to see what my friend was up to. Joe placed a bottle of Coke on the roof of a brand-new Lincoln, bought with reward money, no doubt. In the dim glow of the lot lights, I saw the investigator flip open his coat and draw a pistol out from his belt. No one was around when I saw him load the revolver with a quick snap of a cartridge clip. He did it too fast. I wasn't impressed, but then I wasn't big on guns. I was a whip whiz—a legacy from my young years on a New Mexico ranch. "I can do more with a buggy whip than a monkey can do with ten feet of grapevine," I bragged to whoever would listen.

Several sunrises passed. Then I found myself with Martha and Joe in a rented Fairlane, headed for the high plains of West Texas. Martha MacAnally, a *Dallas Times Herald* newswoman, was the target of a lot of back-alley news talk. A female reporter on the news side was a rare bird. Women in journalism were supposed to do their thing in the society section. Martha busted her butt to get a position as a reporter with the males on the news or editorial side of the business. She cared nothing about being a "woman's writer." She accepted all the back-page story assignments without a gripe.

Male reporters would have bitched all day if they had to cover Japanese Boy Scouts arriving at a Grand Prairie airport for a visit to a Texas ranch. She, in her own words, "didn't give a rat's ass" what the work was, as long as it "wasn't rewriting wedding announcements." And, Martha will remind you, she made a hell of a story out of the Japanese kids' visit, especially when they jumped out of the plane, ceremoniously and thoughtlessly planting the Rising Sun flag on American soil. You guessed it: they weren't even born when American blood was spilled at Pearl Harbor. The article made the front page with a picture. With that same determination, Martha convinced her managing editor that she needed a "home run," a really great story. This missile story might be it.

As I watched her in the rear-view mirror, I could see why she usually got her story or her way. She had those eyes that are often described as "pools." They were the kind of eyes that promised in the daylight what was not about to be delivered at night. Martha was using them at this juncture to "thank" Joe for his generosity in asking her to come along. I could only admire her face, complete with a cute set of dimples. She would die if she heard her facial features described in the "cute" vernacular. Actually, though, one of the guys on the *Herald* rewrite desk remarked that "she has the face of an angel and the heart of a burglar."

I was enjoying watching her spin her web around the handsome Mr. Drum. An hour later, he saw the sign indicating that Plainview was in sight, with Tulia and Happy not far ahead.

Joe said that he needed to get some "tools" and suggested a drive to Happy to supply the need. Every town of any size in West Texas has two institutions: a post office where the government checks can be disbursed in the event of a crop failure, and a hardware store that has tools to fix broken machinery when the bleached ground finally yields a crop. City planners mapping out this part of town wisely put the post office right next to the hardware store. When Joe returned, the items he had in a sack might have been tools or equipment down on the farm, but in the

135

city they were more often called "burglar tools." Another hop and the tool man was back in the Fairlane. I whipped around in the middle of the street, catching sight of a store clerk jotting down what was probably the license plate of a Ford suspiciously fleeing down the main drag.

"I really aced him when I asked if he had change for a hundred-dollar bill. Guess it's not every day that a stranger comes in that feller's place and plops down cash for a hammer and a chisel and a crowbar. Maybe it was the flashlight I needed that set the fella's mind to working. Guess he has visions of becoming Happy's next hero. A rural Dick Tracy, I 'spose," Joe said as he watched out the back window for any signs of a chase. "Sure wish we could hang around 'til the trace on this license is back. The sheriff is gonna kick the guy's ass when the registration comes back as a rental to the Treasury Division of the Secret Service. Can't hurt to rent one more car on my old government credit card."

We reached Tulia and headed east on Highway 1318, an easy drive on the flat, dry land. Suddenly, in the featureless landscape, we saw a pasture full of Quonset huts to the right of the road. There were nine half-round tin buildings, huts just like those in the World War II movies. When American flyers went to England, all of the airmen were assigned to those little huts. They were quick to build and easy to maintain. What were they doing here? GI surplus? Doubtful. These on the high plains looked like they were built for stateside use. They were ugly but useful for storing missiles.

"Which one's ours?" I asked nonchalantly, slowing the Ford to a creep. There was silence as Joe studied the field. There was no activity in sight. "Need some time to guess, Joe?" I teased him. "Joe, Joe. Are you asleep?"

Joe was paralyzed. It had been a year since he'd last laid eyes on the property and he hadn't paid too much attention even then. "Damn! Nothing looks familiar. Damn, I can't remember!"

Martha caught my eye in the rear-view mirror. "I think we'd do as well to get on up the road to Plainview. Good, clean place to do some clear thinking," I said.

Martha chimed in. "I hear tell they'll give you an extra splash of cream gravy with the chicken-fried steaks." Her lighthearted remarks faded as she turned her head to see a big sign on the edge of the property: "ANYONE FOUND ON THIS PROPERTY AFTER DARK WILL BE SHOT!" The printing was clear.

"That might not kill my appetite," I tried to joke, "but it sure might tighten me up too much for peach cobbler!" Martha giggled nervously.

Supper was much better than expected. The waitress, Plainview's football queen just ten years ago, brought extra cream gravy and winked at Joe. Despite the good food, we just sorta' picked at the evening's offerings. Our reluctance to dive in and devour our meals drew an "Everything all right here?" from the waitress. She wet a stump of a pencil on her tongue as she totaled the ticket. A big tip assured her that there wasn't anything wrong with the food or the service.

The day was slipping away as we motored north again. The western horizon displayed a light show with a Sherwin-Williams sunset at center stage. A brilliantly painted orange Cap Rock sky faded to turquoise as it slipped under a canopy of royal purple. By the time we reached our target area, darkness had settled over the compound of oval tin huts. A few friendly lights from nearby farmhouses winked at the darkness. The wind, incessantly tormenting the dusty land, ceased blowing just for a little while.

"What a great night for missile chasing!" Joe said. With renewed attitude and vigor, he cradled his tools and a very large flashlight, ready for the fact-finding mission. Once he located the target, he would summon us, and we could document our discoveries on film. Joe dove from the car with the vigor of an airborne paratrooper and disappeared into the inky blackness of the night.

Slowly, with Martha now at the wheel, our lone auto prowled the dirt roads ringing the project. With the sun gone and no moonlight bathing the countryside, there was comfort in the darkness.

As planned, Martha and I coasted near the southeast corner of the Quonset compound. No lights. No brakes. Just coasting. Joe was to rendezvous with us at the site in thirty minutes. Exactly thirty minutes later, Joe jumped back into the rear seat, out of breath. He huffed and puffed that he had knocked locks off three huts but found nothing. He needed a breather. After setting the coordinates for the next meeting, he was off again.

Back in the darkness, the wind was getting a little frisky, increasing the puffs of twirling dust. Outlaw wheat stalks in the shallow ditch along the roadside were swaying to the rhythm of the night breeze. An errant tumbleweed danced across the headlights, now a safe distance from the project.

The boredom of waiting was interrupted when I suddenly caught sight of lights. Not farmhouse lights, but rather car lights entering the hut area! I swung around so I could get a better look out the back window. Ridiculously, I thought of that warning sign.

"Whaddya see?" Martha asked, no sensuous purr in her voice now. "What's happening? Is Joe in trouble? Are we in trouble?" Her voice cracked a little. "Let's turn this pony around and get Joe. I'm heading for the huts!"

"And headed for trouble," I whispered to my reflection in the side window. With the lights off, there was no shape to the road. I rolled down my passenger window. If we were still on the road, we would hear the sound of gravel crunching beneath the tires. The lights that invaded the Quonset quarters were now behind one of the structures, casting a halo over the property. Martha let the car roll slowly toward the compound, not daring to touch the brakes that, if tapped, would paint the countryside with red light.

Eight or ten minutes passed. Then the visitor's lights backed away from the compound and onto the entrance road as the car slowly moved toward the brighter lights of downtown Tulia.

Martha eased down on the gas and flicked on the dashboard switch, bathing the road in light. But where was Joe? Two trips around the entire project failed to provide an answer. Then, like an apparition, Joe crawled out of the darkness and pulled himself into the back seat. He looked like he had fought three rounds with a hay baler and lost. "Anybody got a rag? I'm getting blood all over this back seat. Cut my hand all to hell!" He may not have been bleeding to death, but blood on a rental car always draws unnecessary concern.

Without any encouragement, Joe babbled as he tried to catch his breath. "I'm whacking and cracking on those damned locks. That Master Deluxe is a killer. I got our huts down to three. I thought you all would probably go nuts when those car lights switched from the road to the compound. I know I did! Geez! I knew in my insides it wasn't you... Before the lights hit me, I just leaped! Hell, I jumped into the darkness. Deepest darkness I ever dove into. It felt like ten feet deep. Crap! I landed on Lord knows what…a set of bedsprings? A car body? A hell of a lot of cans. I thought I'd jumped into a damned garbage pit. I hit the hard stuff and started crawling. It seemed like those lights were right above me." Joe was wiping blood and trying to repair some damaged places on his new leather coat.

"Main thing is, I don't think they made us. I think they only examined one of the buildings, and that was one that I hadn't busted the lock on. Have no idea what brought them out on a night like this. Might have been just a night watchman. I couldn't tell. I didn't ask." He smiled, winking to Martha over his little joke.

Joe thought the next hut he hit would have the "mother lode" in it. "Bert, ya wanna bring your equipment and be ready when I pop the lock?"

"Might as well. We're halfway there. Martha, let us commandos out."

The wind was now kicking up to West Texas strength. The lock on the seventh hut was a snap, but prairie grass growing in the door track made it a little tough and noisy to open. At least there were no lights approaching.

The spacious Quonset building smelled like old dust. In the dark, shapes came to life when hit with the camera light, like monuments in a remembrance park. There were aisles between big cabinets and little cabinets, as well as lots of stuff that meant nothing to me. I saw massive, dusty machinery, hard to photograph without panning from one end to the other. I crawled between the units. I filmed plates with labels and numbers. I shot pictures with my still camera. I was totally focused, doing what I came to do. Shoot the pictures. Get the story. No time to work up a scare. I shot everything I could, but I was none the wiser about what I was shooting.

Until that point, I had not given any thought to the idea that I was breaking and entering. Of course, this is how good newsmen operate. A reporter can work only with total concentration. The instant is paramount. Any diversion throws the mind off-course. I was squeezing my way between a couple of cabinets when I heard a sound like a door sliding. It spooked me. "What ifs" started whirring through my mind.

Then it occurred to me that this caper was a case of breaking and entering. Maybe the station would take up for me. Like hell. My bosses didn't even know I was out prowling. Really scared now, I worked my way to open space. "What's with it?" I whispered over the unholy noise of a now howling wind mixing with some loose tin.

Almost irritated that he had to explain, Joe said, "Ah, I was checking name plates on some equipment in the back there and knocked over a cover from one of those big somma bitches. Scared the shit out of me."

"Me too," I huffed a big breath of dust and muffled a sneeze into my coat sleeve. With my allergies, dust was one of my worst enemies.

I finished exposing all of the film I had with me. Both cameras were now empty. I had lot of pictures of…what? Something? Nothing? No, it was something. It was important. A lot of the stuff there looked like it had never been used. It was uncrated, but it had never seen action. We left.

Martha was inside the getaway car, bouncing up and down like a schoolgirl at a rally. Sliding into the car, I let out a war whoop. "Somma bitch!" Martha wanted to know every minute detail. We were delighted to fill her in, with an embellishment or two for local color.

The trek back to Lubbock was quick. We parked the rented Ford for the night on the back lot of the Holiday Inn, away from prying eyes. We agreed that a toast to an evening well spent was in order, even if it was lifted in the motel's ambitiously named "Entertainment Center."

As we exited the car and I closed the door, my eye caught Joe's movements in the back seat. Slipping his pistol from its convenient place under his belt, Joe shoved it down between the back seats. I knew that, in Texas, no pistols were allowed in a drinking place. But Joe had been packing it in the missile barn. Would he have drawn it if there had been an intrusion? It was not a thought worth thinking.

In the cantina, a colorful, aging jukebox with decorative bubbles whined an unknown tune. A green Coke bottle clinked with a cold Pearl long neck and a tumbler of Scotch on ice as we congratulated one another. Someone said, "Here's to a job done. Maybe not well, but done." With a napkin, Joe mopped blood from another hurt place. Finally, we repeated and mentally catalogued all of the details completing the evening's story.

I was the first to say that the Pearl made me sleepy, thinking regretfully that Joe would now have the field—and Martha—to himself. And Martha, who'd had her notebook out for some time, was still scratching notes. "I'll have one more drink to make sure those Scottish whiskey makers stay employed and then call it -30-."

Back in Dallas, it took four days to round up what we now called a "missile posse" to evaluate the pictures and the situation. Experts from Texas Instruments, Collins Radio and Chance Vought were invited to view the film. After hearing my description of the entire adventure, they were anxious to see what our films and pictures would bring to light.

The film room was loaned by Gordon Older, an independent film operator in Dallas who could fix you up with a Brownie Hawkeye or all of the gear for filming a moon shot. I apologized for the cramped quarters, explaining that I was not ready to have my Channel 8 television bosses view this project.

Scene after scene brought ooh's and ahh's from the three guest experts. Well into the film of the missile system, the TI engineer tapped the Collins fellow on the arm. "Damned thing was sure as hell not demilitarized, was it?"

"Looks like it just came out of the crate."

"Looks like it's just off the assembly line, before salvagers got it." said the Vought engineer. The engineers asked that the film be run over again and again.

Martha whispered to me that she was "way ahead of the experts." She had already written the story. She just needed to fill in the blanks. "It's not my style to write ahead," Martha said, "but I have already researched the background of the Tulia Titan, and he is a bag of tricks. I'm ready to give him a ride he'll never forget."

After an hour, the judges called for a discussion. "We'd better all sit down for this one," the Collins man directed. Seated on boxes and nail kegs, each man told why there was a problem if they exposed the farmer on any other charge than failure to demilitarize the missile launcher.

In detailed explanations, the engineers said that it all boiled down to one element, one vital fixture. "There was no gyroscope," the Collins man said. "Without a gyroscope, the missile system has no way to guide a missile through the launching sequence. It would likely as not take off, zoom around and come back to land in your lap."

They had nice words for the thoroughness of the photography. "Great film. It shows everything. Good investigative work."

"You might want to get the feds to pursue a case against him on theft or something like that," the Vought engineer said.

Then Joe Drum, the father of the caper, appeared at the door of the screening room and was introduced. Turning to me, he added a logical thought: "If we take after this guy—if *you* take after this guy—he might turn around and get you for breaking into his place. And if the case is tried out in West Texas, you sure as hell ain't gonna win in that court with that jury."

After the experts left, Martha said that she was going to the Press Club and possibly "get wasted." With a smile, she invited Joe Drum to chauffeur her. She told me to call her sometime and said, "Thanks for the tip." I gave her my best *de nada* and *hasta luego*.

The Day Kennedy Died

It was early on Friday morning, and showers had washed the city overnight. The cloud curtain hadn't drawn back enough to let the sun spring forth. In fact, the dull orange oval looked like an egg encased in cement dust. Later the sun would reign supreme. Now the sky was gray.

I was dodging traffic down South Central Expressway. It was not as heavy as usual, and I lowered the window of the sports unit that I had taken home Thursday night.

My mind was pleasantly blank. I had no plans for the weekend—just get President Kennedy and his cronies out of town. Vice President Lyndon Johnson and the other Texas Democrats had the chief executive in Texas for a visit. A few political fences needed mending. Politics were okay, but they didn't matter much to me. An early morning AM radio station was reporting that the *Dallas Morning News* ran a full-page ad by some obscure committee chastising the president and urging him to do this or that.

I whipped down Ross Avenue to avoid the heavy traffic on Pacific. I was glad that our station fathers had located the new headquarters in the southwest end of downtown, avoiding a lot of midtown tie-ups. I turned on Lamar. As I passed by the Texas Bank, I reminded myself that I needed to check on what was developing around Main and Commerce.

I thought that there might be a story there. Some old man by the name of Semiotte was buying a lot of that neglected property. I had a tip that the old, seedy land buyer in the rumpled suit was a front for W.W. Overton, who wanted to develop the central west end into something called One Main Place. I would check into that Monday.

When I passed Main Street, I realized that it was still too early for the crowds that would line the street about noon in anticipation of the presidential motorcade. Weeks ago, a map of the route had been published. The entourage would travel from Love Field down Lemmon to downtown. Main was selected as the crosstown street.

When I reached headquarters, I swung the unit in between the *Morning News* building and the WFAA studios. Then I drove on to the back parking lot. Someone had parked in the space marked for sports; I had the sports unit and, now, no place to park. I pulled over and slipped into the space reserved for the big boss, General Manager Mike Shapiro. He would give the sports man, Charlie Jones, hell.

Dallas was not a Kennedy town, but plans for the visit had been in place a long time. WFAA reporters Tom Alyea and Fred Hatton were already in Fort Worth taking care of the president's overnight visit and morning love fest over steak and toast, a breakfast menu designed to underline the fact that this was where the West began.

Big, husky Dallas photographer Mal Couch was to ride along on the truck carrying the press, a few limousine lengths behind JFK's open Lincoln. The rain had stopped, so the Secret Service, with encouragement from the locals, left the clear bubble-top off. The crowd would have eye contact with the president and his wife. After all, that was why he was here—paying off a political debt. A good peek at the pair was like a signed check to the local Democratic organization.

Bob Walker, the radio guy with the great voice and acute news sense, was the new WFAA news director. He was heading to Love Field to "talk" Kennedy and the executive party off the plane. The event was to be carried live on television. That was a big deal. It was no easy task to set up equipment in off-site locations, especially since covering Kennedy was a pool effort, with all three stations contributing.

As assistant news director, I had all eight WFAA newsmen scattered in strategic places. Then I took my camera and luncheon invitation and trooped off to the Trade Mart, where President and Mrs. Kennedy, Vice President Johnson, Governor John Conally and other VIPs would be shaking hands and dining. There might be some speaking and a chance for quotes.

It's strange to recall that time now. Everyone I ran into seemed to be rather blasé about the affair. Channel 4's camera crews were connecting the last wires and completing tests for the live transmission out of the Trade Mart. Capable Eddie Barker from Channel 4 was handling the on-air chores there. The Trade Mart had a large hall, an appropriate setting for such an affair. I didn't really care about what was to happen. This was just one more big luncheon. But I did appreciate the news story being created to spark a dull Friday. After walking the premises at the Trade Mart, I went back outside, hoping to get a shot of the celebrities making their grand entrances.

I was standing near one of three Dallas detective units when the officer and I heard the police radio squawk something strange. We couldn't make it out. "What's that? Something going on downtown?" I asked.

"Don't know," the cop said, still trying to pick up more monitor traffic, which now turned from orders to commands. "Sounds like someone got hit," the detective said.

"With what—a rock? An egg?" I quipped. Then I got a little more concerned. About that time, Channel 11's Jackie Renfro came moseying around with his usual "What's up?" I shot back, "Not so much what's up, but who's down."

Suddenly, I realized what I'd said. Without another word, Jackie and I started running toward the street as we heard police car and motorcycle sirens screaming from vehicles exiting Stemmons Freeway onto Industrial Boulevard. I tried frantically to film the presidential Lincoln convertibles as soon as they were in sight, but instead of stopping at the Trade Mart, the vehicles whizzed right past the entrance and kept going.

I shouted to Renfro, "Jackie, something's wrong. Something's bad wrong. I didn't see anyone in those limousines but the drivers!" I didn't mention that I thought I saw a foot extended out across the boot of the convertible. As I ran back toward the detective's car, I tried to figure out what was happening, but I just drew a blank. What the hell was happening? I had never come across this sort of action before.

Back in the car, I asked the detective what he was doing or going to do. The cop seemed just as stunned, but he did say that the motorcade was ordered to head for Parkland Hospital. With lights and sirens blinking and wailing, the unmarked car with the detective and I joined a bunch of black-and-white units tearing up the same route. It was only a little more than a mile to the hospital. I jumped out of the car as soon as they reached the semicircular emergency drive dock.

Curiously, no one standing outside the hospital seemed in a hurry or even had a sense of urgency. They were mostly dignitaries who had been in the motorcade vehicles. Senator Ralph Yarborough, one of the lawmakers walking up and down the concrete driveway, was white as a sheet.

"What happened?" I asked him. Yarborough, a longtime senator who could talk a blue streak under any circumstances, was speechless. He opened his mouth and no words came out.

I figured that I was wasting my time outside the emergency entrance. So I took another ten or fifteen feet of pictures showing more stunned faces, including some of the women crying. Then I walked past the two limousines parked at the loading dock. In one vehicle, blood was all over the seats. I lifted my camera and filmed the roses still in a bouquet, just as they'd been presented to Jackie Kennedy at the airport. My hand was unsteady. I was breathless, but in a moment, even though my head was not real clear, I was on automatic pilot.

On the scene of a story, the first thing a reporter does is get in touch with his office. The only phone available was in use by a loudmouthed Washington newsman spitting into the mouthpiece.

"That's enough," I yelled at the correspondent. "Enough! Enough! Enough!" The man on the phone shouted back that he was not about to give up the phone.

"If this local prick [he pointed to me as if the party on the other end of the line could see me] doesn't quit pestering me, I'm gonna shove this phone up his ass!" Then I learned from his report that the president had been shot and the governor seriously wounded.

I was ready to look for a phone in a less occupied area when I saw Sheriff Bill Decker and his deputies. It appeared that they had just left trauma room no. 1, where traffic seemed endless. Too many people to be good news. The sheriff continued toward me. "Sheriff, what does it look like?" I asked, trying to be professional but finding that my throat was tight and my breath short. My heart was racing. The sheriff stopped in his tracks. "Son, have ya ever seen a head-shot deer with the back of the skull missing?" A vivid picture of a very serious situation. That was Decker.

"Sheriff, a person can't live with that. That just don't happen," I said to Decker. I was shocked. The sheriff focused on me. He nodded. His hat went forward and then back up, tight on his head. Now I knew. I was scared, but I found a phone and called the station. After many rings, I got radio newsman John Allen on the other end.

"John, I'm at Parkland." I couldn't catch my breath. "The sheriff just told me that Kennedy has suffered a head wound that he can't possibly live with. You can put that on the radio and say Sheriff Bill Decker indicated that."

"I don't think so," John said.

"Why not?" I was screaming. "He's dead for all practical purposes! Don't you understand?"

"You do it," John related quietly in the same voice he used to announce the time and temperature. "You have the air. Tell 'em what you know." With that he was gone.

I went on the air, live, on WFAA radio. I told what I knew, no more. I did not say that the president was dead. I related that Sheriff Bill Decker led me to believe that President John Kennedy could not live. This was, sadly, the first announcement of the biggest news story of the century.

After I made the phone report, I just sat alone in the hospital conference room. I knew that the machinery of television news would quickly swing into action now in the controlled chaos of trying to cover the nation's biggest story of this, or probably any other, year. But right now I appreciated the silence, though it wasn't really silent. No door was thick enough to keep out the emergency room cacophony on the afternoon of November 22, 1963. But through it all, I tried to collect the thoughts whirling around in my head. I needed to organize them, catalogue them. "What have I done? What remained to be done?" So much to think about.

Instinctively, as assistant news director, I knew that I was needed to help run things back in the newsroom. If anything needed managing, it was a news operation during the time of a presidential murder. At the idea of such a sick thought, I treated myself to a small, private smile—as if this happened every day.

Outside the hospital, there were still a lot of cars, mostly official looking. None appeared to be available for my use. The detective who gave me a lift to Parkland Hospital had left. So I figured that there was nothing left to do but to go to the front of the hospital and stand on my favorite street, Harry Hines Boulevard, and maybe commandeer civilian transportation.

The old man in the aging DeSoto made only one mistake that day. He hadn't locked his passenger-side door. When he stopped for a red light at Harry Hines and Motor, I grabbed the handle, released the latch and jumped inside. I told the startled driver that I was from Channel 8 News. "The president has been shot, and I need a ride to the television station—pronto!"

The fact that this gray-haired citizen announced that he was not going my way was of no consequence at this point. "Let's get going and no detours," I yelled. He mashed hard on the accelerator with his right shoe, shouting, "You are crazy! You are gonna kill us, and where's the brakes?"

Cars and pedestrians gave the DeSoto plenty of right of way as we raced down the street through stoplights with flickering lights and a wildly braying horn, carving our way through traffic. I couldn't get any stations with news on the car radio. Hitting all of the buttons and flipping the knobs only resulted in noise, but no news, as well as a terrified and now very angry driver.

Finally, the petrified driver circled in front of the station and found the brakes. "Thanks! You are the best!" I shouted as I jumped from the car.

Later, I wondered what the man said to his wife when they sat down for supper, and she asked, "And how was your day, Sweetie?" He might tell her about the president being shot by a crazy man. He might tell of giving an insane man a ride to a television station. Who would have believed his crazy day?

In the gleaming white studio with the giant tower out back, there was the organized confusion common around a news operation. Program Director Jay Watson and Jerry Haynes, the kids' show host and staff announcer, had already rounded up as many "grassy knoll" witnesses as they could locate and brought them back to the station. (Cooking show hostess Julie Benell was preempted, prompting her loud objections.) The shooting witnesses were wonderful, describing clearly and in detail the events they witnessed that awful day. They had told their story many times, but each time they managed to make the narration sound fresh and urgent. Days passed before the "ON AIR" sign went dark at WFAA.

Now back at the studio, I found myself performing a complicated juggling act. I needed to get all of the film, including my own, processed and edited while I discussed the events at the Trade Mart and Parkland Hospital with the staff, other news outlets and even the Federal Bureau of Investigation.

One of the odd photo story details of that bizarre day involved Tom Alyea, a reporter/photographer who heard the commotion on the radio as he was returning from Fort Worth in a news unit. At the Texas School Book Depository on Commerce Street, he jerked the emergency brake on his vehicle and raced to the building. Moments later, he was locked in the building shooting pictures when detectives and lab men found the chicken bones from Oswald's lunch, and Detective J.C. Day found Oswald's rifle and held it high over his head. Both incidents made great pictures.

Unfortunately, back at the station, I had a hard time convincing Tom to drop his film from the sixth-floor window to waiting hands below. It would save time from Tom's exiting the building and driving his car to the waiting studio. Finally, Tom dropped the film to his colleague, and the resulting pictures were some of the day's most memorable, without a doubt making Tom a hero that day. In addition to Tom's footage, big Mal Couch got great pictures of people scattering about the scene after the shots scared them.

Some newsmen had stories of missed opportunities. Another Channel 8 reporter, A.J. L'hoste, stood at the intersection of Elm and Houston at the start of the day. No one seemed to be there. The crowd was over on Main Street. So A.J. joined them on Main. Thirty minutes later, Kennedy was shot at Elm and Houston.

In the newsroom, I picked up chatter on the police monitor indicating a shooting across the river in Oak Cliff. A Dallas police officer might be involved. Ron Reiland, the newsroom's navy retiree, was sent to investigate. Yes, it was an officer down, Reiland reported. He said that he was in pursuit with other policemen as they trailed a suspect. The officers and Reiland, along with *Dallas Morning News* reporters Hugh Aynesworth and Jim Ewell, were headed for the Texas Theatre on Jefferson Avenue in Oak Cliff.

In the darkened theater, a seated male drew a pistol and tried to fire at Officer Nick McDonald, who had approached the man and ordered him to surrender. Reiland filmed it all. Outside, he continued filming as the suspect was crammed into a squad car and taken downtown.

Minutes later, Reiland came running into the newsroom, saying, "If this is the guy who killed the officer and maybe shot the president, I may have the Pulitzer Prize!" Reiland didn't always see the difference between hoping and having, so I just said, "Ron, I hope you do."

As it happened, Reiland's happy anticipation was premature. Inside the theater, he had left his sun filter in the camera slot. He didn't get the shot of McDonald grabbing the suspect's pistol and placing his finger and thumb under the hammer. Then, in his excitement, as they emerged from the theater, Reiland removed the filter. The exposed film was dark and unusable from the inside, and hot and ruined outside.

Reiland was the same WFAA reporter assigned to be in the basement of the police station the following Sunday when Jack Ruby shot Lee Harvey Oswald. He didn't make it. He had elected to stay "on the bridge" at the station and command the newsroom—just like a good navy guy.

Before the weekend was over, bizarre events were a dime a dozen. I was shocked when three "suits" (FBI agents) came into the newsroom on Saturday afternoon, wanting some film processed. They said that they didn't have the authority to disclose how important this "project" was.

In the hall next to the editing room, one agent pulled a little box of 8mm film out of his pocket. "You want this film processed?" I asked, thinking that they wanted us to develop somebody's amateur film. "Develop this? No can do. We can only process 16mm. We'd ruin this if we tried. No television station and very few, if any, photo shops can do it either. If it's that important, let me make a phone call and we will do it right."

The agents were very pleased at our taking the initiative. I made a phone call to an acquaintance at Kodak. They would open the lab at Love Field. As the FBI men were leaving, I had a little fun. "Don't let any jake-leg film man try to soup that celluloid in some tomato can." They smiled and left. Apparently, they took my advice. The Zapruder shots of a most terrifying moment in history were preserved forever.

Days later, News Director Bob Walker, who six hours earlier had done such a magnificent job of "talking" President Kennedy off the plane, and then keeping our news on the air from our television studio for hours on end, said, "Let's take a break and get out of this studio."

We took a news unit to the Statler Hilton Hotel, where Bob had a room. Bob spoke to the clerk behind the desk, so when we entered the room a bellman marched in with ice, 7 Up and Canadian Club whiskey. We lifted our glasses and wearily reviewed the past few days. We were agreed that we would never want to cover another assassination. But if we had to, we would do it the same way.

Kennedy's assassination was a momentous event, totally unscripted. Events controlled us and our whole operation. But we felt we did rise to the job. During this national crisis, hour after hour, day after day, Channel 8 provided live coverage, including constant updates for the network. The network and the nation recognized and praised our work. WFAA became the darling of ABC.

Channel 8 had the first film on the air. By the time the other stations had their first films on the air, WFAA had a documentary, a full thirty minutes of scenes from the Fort Worth stop, Couch's motorcade film, Alyea's pictures of the depository gun and lunch bones and my stuff from the hospital.

In the quiet and comfort of the Statler Hilton Hotel, we toasted one another again, the whiskey soaking into tired bones. After a long silence, I felt a little philosophical. "Bob, ya know, we were not only covering the news, we were recording history. But, you know, years from now I think we'll look back and say, 'Hell, we wrote the manual on television news.'"

Bob lazily lifted a glass. Mellow now, but still exhausted, he saluted his assistant news director. "Bert, you do good work!" I agreed, but it felt good to hear it.

The Ladies of the White Rose

The air in the fashionable lounge of the Lang Xang Hotel, stirred slowly by giant, four-bladed fans, was thick with smoke. The laughter of the barmaids and B-girls was loud, but their chatter was more like the twittering of small birds as they spread their charms throughout the murky room. The drinkers were oblivious to the noise. The spooks and other spies puffed on Cuban cigars, while the newsmen and correspondents inhaled stateside cigarettes or blew an occasional puff of marijuana. As the hour grew late, the crowd was rewinding to begin or continue a full evening of frolic.

I was enjoying my newfound supply of eighty-proof Schiedam gin. I swallowed slowly to let the juniper juice slip through my lips and tickle my tongue. That Schiedam was hard to come by at Red Coleman's Liquor there on Dallas's Greenville Avenue. I still had a hard time believing how I lucked out with an assignment that let me carouse the night away halfway around the world. It was a "major" doing.

I was then news director at WFAA-TV, and I was delighted to fill a request from an old friend, Murphy Martin. Once ABC's news anchor and correspondent, he had a deal I couldn't pass up. Murphy asked me to accompany him as the photographer on a Ross Perot "United We Stand" mission to identify prisoners of war in North Vietnam. Martin, who was always a strong newsman, was now putting just as much energy into working for the Perot effort to learn more about the prisoners—maybe even get them freed. Remembering the time when Murphy and I rounded up news on the plains of North Texas, I jumped at the chance.

I was using up the last of my off-duty hours this particular evening, drifting with the crowd to a not-so-nice establishment called the White Rose. The Rose was about as wide open as the city of Vientien. During the day, thousands of pack-laden citizens shuffled on foot about the city, doing their daily errands and chores while Communist soldiers and loyal Royal troops did their deeds in an uneasy and delicately balanced peace. Spies were everywhere and secrets were for sale. It was truly a climate for all kinds of stories.

At the end of the day, though, the glow of the setting sun through the windows of the White Rose was mostly covered by oleander bushes waltzing with a stiff evening breeze. The weak twilight was finally replaced by a fuchsia neon sign show.

CIA spooks crept out of the shadows, metamorphosing as Air America employees. After the day's scary action had been tempered with a few highballs, they didn't mind if you already knew who they were, but you couldn't expect them to help you guess that they were really CIA agents. One aviator from the ghost group brought up an incident from earlier in the day. With three fingers of bourbon in a standard Manhattan glass, he raised the tumbler to his lips. He slugged down a worthy drink and chased it with a drag on a genuine Havana stogie. Then he reared back in one of those Queen chairs with his airman buckle half-boots parked on a beat-up coffee table and told the story of his day.

This aviator said that a few hours earlier, billionaire Perot and a band of correspondents had boarded the guy's aging but reliable C-3 on a fact-finding mission southeast of Vientien, to a place called Pac San. A village of refugees was being quartered there, along the Mekong River. Perot's group hoped that they might uncover some information about American MIAs. Though the group experienced some man-made turbulence from ground action, the trip was made without serious incident. The passengers considered themselves lucky.

As the drinks got stronger and tongues loosened, the Air America pilot continued. Apparently, the plane on the relatively quiet Perot mission was "ventilated," as the pilot delicately put it. After the trip, while mechanics were going over the craft, they discovered that ground fire had made some rather large holes in the fuselage.

Another pilot said that he wasn't surprised. The craft probably took fire as it cleared the end of the Vientien runway. "Usually it's some unfriendly folks down there in the brush. They just want you to know they're in charge of this piece of real estate, even if their kingdom is just an acre at the end of a dirt airstrip." The self-assured pilot said this casually, without even removing his sunglasses. The newsmen passengers just looked at one another.

Several of the news guys thought of what a story that would make if it got out stateside: "Perot escapes enemy fire while on Vietnam prisoner fact-finding mission." The story never made it. The waiting list to use a phone was so long that it took nine hours to place a call to the States.

While stories, like the cigars, were getting shorter as the evening wore on, two other Dallas newsmen and I possessed the best story of all but decided that it was best not to share it. We just ordered another tray of drinks and compared notes on our caper, laughing together as we relived our adventure with one another.

The story began when Hugh Aynesworth, a really good Dallas journalist, heard about two priests fresh from North Vietnam, now staying at the Lang Xang Hotel. They had actually carried out with them a list—a full, official, accurate list—of Americans being held prisoner in the north. No one knew that such a list even existed. This was exactly what Perot wanted.

Acting on this tip, WFAA reporter Gene Thomas, Hugh and I decided to put that information to work. We made our move one afternoon when the priests left their hotel room. A fourth reporter fast-talked the desk clerk out of the clerics' room key. He then stood as lookout. Once inside the room, we frantically searched for the list. In the first place, we didn't know what it looked like. Then we had no idea where it could be. Was it in a drawer? In a Bible? Poking around at a fevered pitch, we were like squirrels searching for nuts. In the middle of this frenzied activity, there was a knock on the door. The search halted, and we looked at one another like coyotes caught in headlights. I was nearest the door, so I grabbed the knob and flung the door open.

A uniformed houseboy stood there, smiling, holding two neatly cleaned and pressed black suits. For men of the cloth, of course. I froze, swallowing hard. If the service person had been more observant, he would have detected from my face that there was some skullduggery afoot. Thinking fast, I pulled a wad of bills from my pocket, enough to cover the bill and a generous tip. My companions in crime silently cheered. The houseboy left happily.

A few minutes later, Hugh found the list. After making certain that no tell-tale marks of search and seizure were apparent, we searched for a duplicating machine. This was not an easy task in the Far East, especially when the material was so secret and its acquisition questionable. Finally, the list was copied and back in its proper place. We had pulled off what our business is all about—fact-finding, first class.

Later, agents from the CIA, the State Department or maybe even Perot's group (we never knew who) secretly scanned the information and profusely praised our "great work" and "wonderful information." But in a disappointing anticlimax, we were never told what happened to the list or who used it. Did Perot ever learn of all the details of the caper? We never knew.

And the priests apparently never knew that the property had been disturbed. They may have thought that free cleaning and pressing were part of room service for men of the cloth. In the end, the only reward we garnered from the escapade was another great story to tell.

Now, with still vivid memories of the "priestly caper," Gene, Hugh and I joined the rest of the White Rose crowd. The stories and the laughter grew more raucous as the night stretched toward dawn.

Other incidents were not as fearsome but rather all too typical of that sad country at that sad time. Our group was on the edge of the dense Laotian jungle when nature called me, real loud. While there were no tigers and other frightful beasts around, there were soldiers on patrol and quite a few refugees exploring their new grounds. Accepting the fact that options were few, I elected to take to the jungle. A short walk led me to a small clearing in the middle of the heavy growth and tangled vines. A few forest noises, probably monkeys or birds, assured me that I was in a private place, away from the civilized world. The problem became apparent when it was time to clean up. It was an issue of convenient tissue. No jungle Charmin on a nearby hook. No corncobs. No sticks or leaves in the clearing.

The answer to the problem was right there in my wallet: currency. Laotian dollars. I had lots of them, and they were quickly recirculated. After the situation was cleared up, I hurried back to the safety of the mission party. But as I reached the edge of the thick jungle foliage, I heard the thunder of footsteps, and turning, I saw two dozen Laotian villagers running toward the "toilet area." Their object: the discarded currency.

The listening crowd at the White Rose didn't think that story was very funny. But they did regard it as hilarious when another correspondent staggered down from one of the fun rooms above the bar. This guy was long known to the B-girls as a "cheap American bastard" because he didn't want to pay the going rates, starting around twenty-five bucks.

On this evening, he had just negotiated a lay in the hay with one of the girls for ten dollars. This wheeler-dealer from Denver was a real smartass. According to him, he had "broken the code." He was about to complete the great American-Laotian trade agreement. Congratulating himself on his negotiating skills, he ascended the stairs to the room and got naked in bed. The lights were out. Then a door opened, and a female figure appeared silhouetted against the glowing entrance. A quick movement and then the door closed. Something made its way to the eager customer spread on the bed. His outstretched arms felt something furry. It was, indeed, furry, and it was quick. With a loud, protesting yowl, the cat leaped from the bed.

About the Author

Bert Shipp is a news-gathering legend. Known and loved throughout U.S. media circles, he is truly one of a kind. His uniquely sharp wit, combined with his unparalleled fifty years of experience in Texas's radio, print and television industries, make him an incredible gift to all who know him. Oh, for a clone.

After being a part of the Texas news industry for five decades, Bert flunked Retirement 101 in 1999. After bidding farewell to his colleagues of many years at his goodbye party ("a grand affair," he says), he received a telephone call from his former Dallas bosses at WFAA-TV Channel 8. They asked, "Any chance you can come help out when we get in a pinch?"

He helped. Two years later, the company figured out that it had paid him a nice sum to quit. An Artesia, New Mexico native, Bert's work history included several years of ditch digging, surveying and fixing flats until he decided he needed an education. He attended New Mexico State University, Abilene Christian College and Southern Methodist University. He also met and married Shan Upham in 1954, a move he considers his smartest. Shan didn't drink, smoke, dance or go to movies on Sunday night. Bert decided she fit his budget. He calls her "his leading lady," since as soon as she met him, "She was leading me to the altar."

His first "real" job at the *Abilene Reporter News* paid thirty dollars a week, a salary that motivated him to move to Dallas and the *Dallas Times Herald*. Bert insists that he was hired in Dallas because they figured he must have been good to have survived the tyranny of working for the *Reporter News'* Ed Wischcamper and Richard (Dick) Tarpley, two of the best in the Texas news business.

Bert's stories were highlighted with daily front-page bylines as he made his mark on the education and police beats at the *Times Herald*. This was the '60s, in the heat of the desegregation turmoil, when the Dallas Independent School District was struggling to adjust to the fast, huge growth of the school system.

Gradually, television news became the focus of his career aspirations, and he moved to Channel 5 in Fort Worth, where James Byron of WBAP-TV was the foremost television journalist of the news industry. After two years with *The Texas News*, Bert left to join WFAA-TV Channel 8, where he worked as news director for many of his forty years there.

Shipp has been honored by many groups. Southern Methodist University awarded him the Medal for Journalistic Achievement, and the University of North Texas inducted him into its Journalism Hall of Honor in 1999. Both the Associated Press and United Press International have recognized Shipp with multiple awards.

Shipp also won several Katie Awards from the Dallas Press Club. He was the only newsman to receive Katie Awards in the same year in different fields. He won one Katie for his human interest newspaper story about the "Texas Howdy," the time-honored custom of giving a small wave to drivers passing by from the opposite direction. That same year, he also won for his writing for the *Homesick Texan*, a newspaper for expatriate Texans living in other states or countries.

One of his proudest moments was when he and his son Brett both won Katie Awards from the Dallas Press Club in 1993, something that no Press Club family had ever done.

Married fifty-seven years, Bert and Shan live in Dallas, where their two sons and four of their seven grandchildren also live. Their daughter and three other grandchildren live in Plano, Texas, a suburb of Dallas.

TV newsman in thick of it to the finish

BOB ST. JOHN

Over the years, I have been privy to some of Bert Shipp's adventurous escapades and too close for comfort at other times during attempts at misspent youth. The guy is a throwback to the hell-raising newsmen of yesterday but also made his mark in the present because of his knowledge and ability.

Oh, sure, there are some who might not care for him, but even they would have to admit that to know Bert is to never forget him. So it's difficult to imagine Bert retiring, which he did recently, after 38 years with Channel 8. He served as assistant news director, news director and, since the mid-1970s, assignments editor. Whatever his title, he'll always be that newsman, out there chasing a story.

He was on the scene for the Kennedy assassination and in the Beatles' dressing room. He interviewed presidents and celebrities and drank too much with John Wayne. He mentioned almost being shot once, and there was that time he rode in a smoking plane without a parachute.

And he was whipped by a lawyer, an accused embezzler, a group of prostitutes and a grandmother. They all resented him minding their business for the sake of a story. He recalls not having a chance against the grandmother.

"I was in court covering a criminal case involving her grandson," he said. "She blindsided me and started beating me with her purse. That was the worst whipping I got."

He was at Parkland Memorial Hospital when President John F. Kennedy died.

"I was one of the 22 guys who were first to announce the president's death over the air," he said with his familiar grin.

Driven by Beatlemania

In the fall of 1964, Bert was hanging around the lobby of Memorial Auditorium, waiting for the Beatles to hold a news conference.

"I saw this cop I knew at the door of their dressing room and politely asked if it was OK if I went inside. He said no. We kept talking, and I told him I'd get his daughter an autograph, and that got me in.

"They were sitting around and laughed at my accent, and we just started talking. Channel 8 had an exclusive."

He once hurried to a crime scene where the police had a guy trapped in a house on Hall Street. Bert maneuvered to get closer and jumped out of his car in time to hear an officer yell for him to duck before he got shot. He managed to get safely under his car until order was restored. Bert called home to tell his wife, Shan, that he'd be late for dinner again.

Shan is from Highland Park, and she and Bert met while they were attending the former Abilene Christian College. Bert had driven trucks, stock cars and an ambulance, run a service station and goodness knows what else in his home state of New Mexico. But in Abilene, he was working and going to school.

"I was a surveyor on Dyess Air Force Base there," he said. "I went back years later and do believe it was sloped. . . . Shan was a good Church of Christ girl who didn't drink, dance, smoke or go to the movies on Sunday. So I figured she was good for my budget. We got married in 1953, and she's put up with me all these years."

Out of parachutes

Then there was that ride in a plane pulling gliders.

"The pilot had released a glider, and I was taking pictures. I noticed smoke; an oil line had busted," Bert said. "I turned to the pilot, and it looked like he was getting ready to bail out. I didn't have a parachute! I figured I couldn't talk him out of the parachute, so I convinced him to try to land, which he successfully did."

Feeling reflective, Bert said he was proud that he was able to make friends wherever he went. He also felt good that he could be a part of letting the public know what was happening behind doors normally closed.

Asked whether he would miss the excitement, the rush of the old days, he admitted he would but said, unlike others, he never really got stressed out.

"You have to have a high IQ to get stressed and feel pressure," he said, grinning. "I loved being a newsman, the stress, pressure, everything that went with it."

We talked for a couple of hours until I mentioned that now, in retirement, he'd have more time to write a book about his experiences. Naturally, this could make a lot of people nervous if he told everything. But don't worry, it would make Bert nervous, too.

Visit us at
www.historypress.net